PEP

Ability Test

Practice Book 1

Sarah Collins, Peter Francis, Andrew Hammond,
David E Hanson, Alison Head, Steve Hobbs,
Louise Martine, Chris Pearce

Every effort has been made to trace all copyright holders, but if any have been inadvertently overlooked, the Publishers will be pleased to make the necessary arrangements at the first opportunity.

Although every effort has been made to ensure that website addresses are correct at time of going to press, Hachette Learning cannot be held responsible for the content of any website mentioned in this book. It is sometimes possible to find a relocated web page by typing in the address of the home page for a website in the URL window of your browser.

Hachette UK's policy is to use papers that are natural, renewable and recyclable products and made from wood grown in well-managed forests and other controlled sources. The logging and manufacturing processes are expected to conform to the environmental regulations of the country of origin.

To order, please visit www.hachettelearning.com or contact Customer Service at education@hachette.co.uk / +44 (0)1235 827827.

ISBN: 978 1 3983 8845 1

© Sarah Collins, Peter Francis, Andrew Hammond, David E Hanson, Alison Head, Steve Hobbs, Louise Martine, Chris Pearce 2025

First published in 2025 by

Hachette Learning,

An Hachette UK Company

Carmelite House

50 Victoria Embankment

London EC4Y 0DZ

www.hachettelearning.com

Impression number   10 9 8 7 6 5 4 3 2 1

Year   2027 2026 2025

The authorised representative in the EEA is Hachette Ireland, 8 Castlecourt Centre, Dublin 15, D15 XTP3, Ireland (email: info@hbgi.ie)

All rights reserved. Apart from any use permitted under UK copyright law, no part of this publication may be reproduced or transmitted in any form or by any means, electronic or mechanical, including photocopying and recording, or held within any information storage and retrieval system, without permission in writing from the publisher or under licence from the Copyright Licensing Agency Limited. Further details of such licences (for reprographic reproduction) may be obtained from the Copyright Licensing Agency Limited, www.cla.co.uk.

Cover illustration by Heather Clarke, D'Avila Illustration Agency

Illustrations by Vian Oelofsen and Stéphan Theron

Typeset in FS Albert 15 on 17pt by IO Publishing

Printed in the UK by Bell and Bain Ltd, Glasgow

A catalogue record for this title is available from the British Library.

Contents

Sections

Section 1 Word analogies 5

Section 2 Spot the difference 10

Section 3 Choose a word to fit the space 14

Section 4 Statement logic 22

Section 5 Essential part 33

Section 6 Words in a sequence 37

Section 7 Number sequences 45

Section 8 Number analogies 52

Maths workouts

Maths workout 1 59

Maths workout 2 60

Maths workout 3 62

Maths workout 4 64

Practice papers

About the practice papers 65

Practice paper 1 66

Practice paper 2 81

Practice paper 3 95

Practice paper 4 110

Exam tips and guidelines 123

Section 1 — Word analogies

> **Skills notes**
> - *Word analogy:* to identify the link or connection between groups or pairs of words.

Working with groups of words

An **analogy** is where a link is made between two words; the same analogy can then be applied to a different set of words. When working with groups of words:

i. **spot the connection** and then **apply** it to the second set of words

ii. look at both analogies to find the answer, since homonyms are often used. For example:

> **Select the word that completes the sentence**
> Cap is to (lid, hat, (head)) as sock is to ((foot), shoe, wool).

Working it out

The keyword 'cap' can have several meanings and uses:

Cap	the cap on a container (noun)
	to cap something, or limit it (verb)
	a cap worn on your head (noun)

The second keyword, 'sock', is something worn on your foot, so this analogy involves the third meaning of cap – something you wear.

> **Tip**
> When words have more than one meaning, you can often become distracted and look for the wrong links, so always begin by considering all the meanings of each word.

Section 1 Word analogies

Working with pairs of words

Sometimes the question will give you one analogy and then ask you to find a similar one.

In these cases, you will need to choose the word from a list of possible answers. For example:

> Brave is to cowardly as loathe is to ….
> A heroic   B (adore)   C dislike   D glad

Working it out

In this example, the keyword 'brave' is linked to 'cowardly' because they are opposites (or antonyms). So, using the same analogy, the opposite of 'loathe' (to hate) is 'adore'.

Warm-up activity

Select the word from the brackets that completes the sentence. Circle the correct answers.

1. Bag is to (collect, tools, carry) as pot is to (paint, cup, dig).

2. Subject is to (object, monarch, lesson) as student is to (teacher, class, success).

3. Research is to (cure, hospital, scientist) as study is to (exam, paper, pass).

Find the association between the first pair of words and identify the same relationship with the third word provided. Circle the correct answer.

4. Broom is to sweep as cloth is to ….
   A cotton   B mend   C polish   D material

5. Grow is to food as inflate is to ….
   A tyre   B air   C price   D deflate

6. Ditch is to drop as retain is to ….
   A send   B keep   C reach   D hole

Word analogies

Just for fun

Synonyms

Circle the word that means the **same, or nearly the same**, as the word in bold.

For example:								
distort	A	inform	B	exhibit	C	debate	D	(warp)

1	**string**	A	strain	B	long	C	cord	D	tie
2	**genuine**	A	solid	B	real	C	clever	D	safe
3	**shiny**	A	cold	B	glossy	C	mirror	D	sun
4	**tale**	A	story	B	fairy	C	book	D	wand
5	**scarce**	A	afraid	B	poor	C	fierce	D	scant
6	**supple**	A	loose	B	thin	C	flexible	D	light
7	**stationary**	A	envelope	B	staple	C	glue	D	fixed
8	**tangle**	A	busy	B	knot	C	hair	D	comb
9	**speak**	A	sound	B	word	C	talk	D	loud
10	**road**	A	home	B	address	C	street	D	map

Section 1 Word analogies

Antonyms

Look at each keyword in the first column. Use the word bank to help you choose the word that means the opposite and write it in the final column. The first one has been done for you as an example.

	Keyword	Word bank	Antonym
11	find	search, lost, lose, late	lose
12	dark	light, day, shadow, shine	
13	poor	pale, wealthy, money, match	
14	slow	plod, rapid, race, speed	
15	multiply	more, count, some, divide	
16	release	free, prisoner, find, capture	
17	calm	rest, rush, angry, agitated	
18	sharp	edge, point, rough, blunt	
19	expert	practice, novel, new, novice	
20	freeze	liquid, thaw, ice, dilute	

Challenge

In each group below, all three words are related, except one. Circle the word that does not belong and explain why.

1 volcano   mountain   river
Why? _____

2 pencil   pen   paint
Why? _____

3 thunder   whistle   lightning
Why? _____

Word analogies

Worksheet 1

Let's start

Select the word from the brackets that completes the sentence. Circle each word.

1 Green is to (glass, grass, tree) as blue is to (sky, pool, air). ...../2

2 Fur is to (soft, warm, cat) as scales are to (shiny, fish, weigh). ...../2

3 Finger is to (hand, point, nail) as toe is to (line, shoe, foot). ...../2

4 Ice is to (water, skate, cold) as fire is to (hot, burn, yellow). ...../2

Level up

Circle the word or letter which best completes each statement.

5 Night is to dark as day is to …. ...../1
   A school   B wake   C light   D early

6 Fish is to swim as bird is to …. ...../1
   A fly   B feather   C tree   D poultry

7 Peel is to orange as shell is to …. ...../1
   A sea   B egg   C fish   D crumb

8 Nose is to smell as ear is to …. ...../1
   A lobe   B hear   C loud   D wax

9 Gate is to fence as door is to …. ...../1
   A wall   B lock   C handle   D knob

10 Milk is to cheese as flour is to …. ...../1
    A mill   B wheat   C farm   D bread

   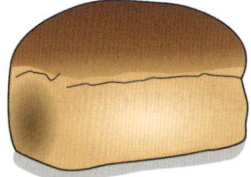

Record your score ...../14

Section 2 Spot the difference

> **Skills notes**
> - *Spot the difference:* to identify the word that does not belong in the group by finding a pattern.
>
> **For example:**
>
> Three of the words in the list are related to each other in some way. Find the word that is not linked to the others.
>
> kick   throw   catch   (ball)

Identify the word class

Unlike synonym and antonym questions, 'spot the difference' questions usually contain just **one word class**, such as nouns. The trick is to find out why one word <u>does not fit</u> with the other three words and so is the odd one out.

A typical question could list a group of animals, for example, cat, bird, hamster, fish. All the animals are pets, but only one lives in water, so the fish is the odd one out.

Working it out

In the example in the skills notes above, all the words are connected with sports so this is the common theme.

Kick, throw and *catch* are all verbs (actions) but *ball* is a noun (a thing). This means that *ball* is the odd one out.

> **Tip**
>
> Some words can have dual meanings, for example, *to drive* (verb) and *a drive* (noun).
>
> The trick is to focus on the common word class and the meaning that links the other words in the group.

Spot the difference

Warm-up activity

Three of the words in the list are related to each other in some way.
Write the odd one out on the line provided.

1 meat   vegetables   food   fruit   ....
2 desk   whiteboard   paper   keyboard   ....
3 turn   accelerate   indicate reverse   ....

Circle the word that does not belong with the other three in these sets of words.

4 A wipe   B clean   C soap   D wash
5 A running   B gasping   C sprinting D dashing
6 A house   B bungalow   C castle   D accommodation

   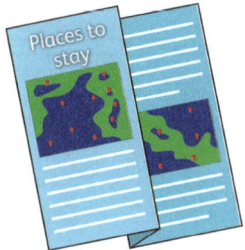

7 Read the list of words. Decide whether each one is a noun (a thing) or a verb (an action). Write the words under the correct heading.

elephant   whisper   basket   sprint   mountain   blink
desert   gallop   volcano decorate ladder   swim

Nouns	Verbs

Section 2 Spot the difference

Just for fun

Matching features

Look at the first two pictures and select one of the options that belongs to the same set.

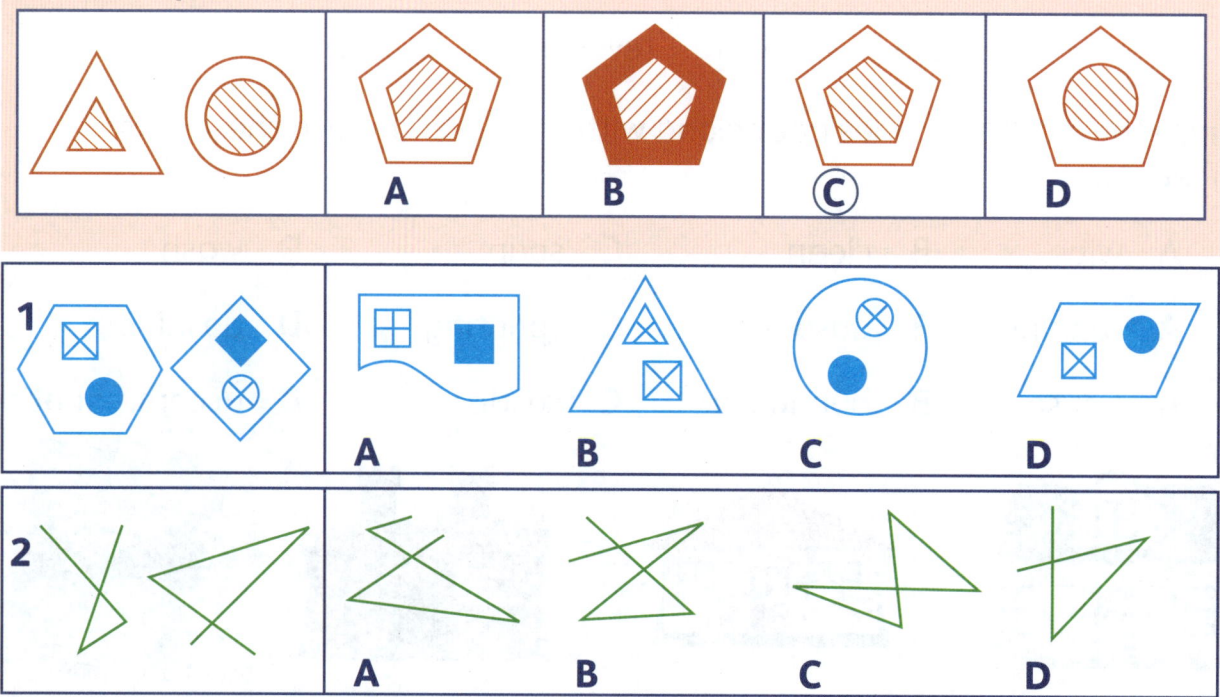

Challenge

Below is a list of words related to Jamaica's culture, geography and lifestyle.

1   Sort the words into the correct categories:

Food and drink	Places and landmarks	Music and culture	Activities and traditions

Reggae   ackee   jerk chicken   Dunn's River Falls

patois   calypso   Blue Mountains   Kingston   patty

cricket   Rastafari   bamboo   Maroon   goat curry

ska   tourism   river rafting   Montego Bay   steel pan

Worksheet 2

Circle the word that does not belong to the group.

1	A apple	B pear	C orange	D carrot		..../1

2	A lion	B tiger	C wolf	D leopard		..../1

3 A sister   B aunt   C mother   D cousin   ..../1
4 A Monday   B Friday C April   D Sunday   ..../1
5 A wander   B walk   C stroll   D fly   ..../1
6 A silver   B green   C gold   D bronze   ..../1
7 A brook   B river   C stream   D lake   ..../1
8 A barrier B rail   C fence   D door   ..../1
9 A myth   B fable   C fact   D legend   ..../1
10 A find   B acquire C buy   D purchase ..../1

Record your score ..../10

Section 3 Choose a word to fit the space

Skills notes

- *Choose a word to fit the space:* to find the word that makes the sentence complete and logical.

  For example:

  Select the words that complete the sentence.

  Libraries are <u>quiet</u> places for <u>students</u> to study.

  A quiet; student's   **B** quietly; student's

  C quiet; students   **D** quietly; students

Looking at context

These types of items look at how words work together in the context of the sentence. You are asked to look at a sentence with two missing words, then to pick a word from a selection that completes the sentence in a way that makes sense.

You will have practised working out unfamiliar words in English comprehension by reading around the text. This is just another way to test the same thing. Occasionally, you may not understand all the words you are given but do not worry, there will be other clues in the sentence to direct you to the right answer!

Sometimes the words may be more familiar, in which case you may be expected to look at the grammar or word classes more closely.

Working it out

In the example in the skills notes, you are given four possible options. One pair is the correct answer.

Begin by identifying the word classes or function:

quiet – adjective   student's – (possessive) noun

quietly – adverb   students – (plural) noun

Read the whole sentence. We can see that, for it to make sense, a word (an adjective) is needed to give more information about the kind of place and another (a noun) to show who or what visits it.

Warm-up activity

> **Tip**
>
> You can confirm your answer by using each pair of words in a sentence to see which fits best. Only one of them will make sense.
> Always be on the lookout for the following:
> - plural versus possessive nouns
> - regular nouns and verbs versus irregular nouns and verbs
> - homophones versus homonyms versus homographs
> - tenses
> - spelling.

1 Complete the table below.

Word	Explanation	Used in a sentence
plain	• unadorned, simple, easy to understand • large, flat land with few trees	1. .... 2. Cows are grazing on the plain.
plane	....	....

Section 3 Choose a word to fit the space

Word	Explanation	Used in a sentence
rational	....	....
rationale	• guiding principles or beliefs	....
they're	....	....
their	....	The twins got their wanderlust from their parents.
there	....	....

Choose a word to fit the space

2 Circle the correct word in each sentence.

a) Several witnesses (corroborated, collaborated) the victim's report of the incident.

b) There are no medals for (forth, fort, fourth) place in this competition.

c) It is (quite, quiet) obvious that Jillian enjoys maths and science.

d) You will need to (pore, pour, poor) more liquid in that cement mixture to get the right consistency.

e) (Hoards, Hordes) of people descended on the store when they heard there was a 70% sale on electronic items.

Section 3 Choose a word to fit the space

Just for fun

Synonyms and antonyms

Use the words in Table 1 to answer questions 1 to 5. Then use the words in Table 2 to answer questions 6 to 10.

Table 1

flexible	reduce	thrilled	expand	strengthen
shrink	support	rigid	devise	successful
strength	valueless	worthless	pliable	boastful
create	modest	sorrowful	cheerful	enthusiastic
humble	shrink	lucky	valuable	miserable

1 Find the two words that are synonyms for the word 'supple'.

....

2 Find the two words that are synonyms for the word 'unhappy'.

....

3 Find the two words that are antonyms for the word 'undermine'.

....

4 Find the two words that are synonyms for the word 'excited'.

....

5 Find the two words that are antonyms for the word 'vain'.

....

18

Choose a word to fit the space

Table 2

boarder	territory	silly	frontier	foolish
gather	retreat	assemble	flee	proceed
capture	release	flea	staid	gratitude
liberate	kind	exonerate	disperse	aggravate
malicious	exacerbate	vindictive	border	vindicate

6 Find the two words that are synonyms for 'absurd'.

    ....

7 Find the two words that are synonyms for 'collect'.

    ....

8 Find the two words that are antonyms for 'advance'.

    ....

9 Find the two words that are antonyms for 'detain'.

    ....

10 Find the two words that are synonyms for 'cruel'.

    ....

Challenge

Read each clue carefully. Choose two words from Table 2 that best fit the clue, then fill in the blanks.

1 These two words both mean something crazy or ridiculous.

   _____ and _____

2 These two words both mean to bring things or people together.

   _____ and _____

3 These two words mean the opposite of moving forward.

   _____ and _____

Section 3 Choose a word to fit the space

Worksheet 3

Select the most appropriate pair of words to complete the sentence.

1. … playing such loud music at this … . ..../1
   - A whose; hour
   - B whose; our
   - C who's; hour
   - D who's; our

2. Only ten … tickets are … for tonight's concert. ..../1
   - A complimentary; allowed
   - B complementary; allowed
   - C complementary; aloud
   - D complimentary; aloud

3. The … logo must be printed on all … . ..../1
   - A companies; stationary
   - B companies; stationery
   - C company's; stationary
   - D company's; stationery

4. The … said that there are … many instances of truancy for the term. ..../1
   - A principle; two
   - B principle; too
   - C principal; two
   - D principal; too

5. Blue house … the scoreboard all morning but it seems they will … the sport's day after all. ..../1
   - A lead; loose
   - B led; lose
   - C lead; lose
   - D led; loose

6. You can … that he is … from his attitude to the discussion. ..../1
   - A imply; uninterested
   - B imply; disinterested
   - C infer; uninterested
   - D infer; disinterested

7. Do you want to … a different outfit, or … this one? ..../1
   - A buy; altar
   - B buy; alter
   - C by; altar
   - D by; alter

Choose a word to fit the space

8 Jonathan … in Cassie's business and now there is barely any … between them. …/1

   A medalled; piece   **B** medalled; peace

   C meddled; peace   **D** meddled; piece

9 The hospital now offers vegetarian options for … who do not eat …. …/1

   A patients; meet   **B** patience; meat

   C patience; meet   **D** patients; meat

10 There is … graffiti at the … of the statue. …/1

   A new; base   **B** knew; base

   C new; bass   **D** knew; bass

Record your score …/10

Section 4 Statement logic

Skills notes

- *Statement logic:* to identify the statement that must be true based on the facts provided.

For example:

Chen, Joseph and Kiyana are studying wildlife in Jamaica.

Chen always records sightings of birds and insects.

Joseph only records animals he sees near rivers.

Kiyana sometimes records lizards but never records birds.

If the above statements are true, this must mean that only one of the following statements can be true. Which one?

A Kiyana always records birds found near rivers.

B Chen might record insects found near a river.

C Joseph never records lizards.

D Chen and Kiyana both record the same animals.

Deductive reasoning

'Statement logic' questions provide you with a list of statements to read carefully. They then challenge you to find one more true statement in a set of answer choices, based on these facts.

Even though questions like these may seem confusing, if you work through them logically, you will find there can only be one answer that can be true.

Answer choices will be included that distract you, especially when they sound like they could be true, so always focus on the evidence and deal in facts only.

Statement logic

Working it out

Think carefully about the information provided in the three introductory statements in the skills notes. These are facts. You will now be asked to choose which of the following statements, based on the facts you have about Chen, Joseph and Kiyana, must be true (not 'might be true' or 'sound quite possible').

Let's deal with each.

Kiyana always records birds found near rivers.	This can't be true because we are told that Kiyana never records birds, no matter where they are.
Chen might record insects found near a river.	Chen records insects regardless of where they are. So if an insect is near a river, she would still record it.
Joseph never records lizards.	This might be true, but we don't know for sure. If lizards live near rivers, Joseph might record them. There's not enough information to decide.
Chen and Kiyana both record the same animals.	Kiyana never records birds, but Chen always does. So their records can't be the same.

> **Tip**
>
> Always read the question!
>
> Try putting the information you have been given into a table or diagram, as this can help you to spot the true statement more easily. For this example, you could list the people in the statements down one side, then the activities and likes across the top:
>
> | | Records birds | Records insects | Records river animals | Records lizards |
> |---|---|---|---|---|
> | Chen | ✔ | ✔ | | |
> | Joseph | | | ✔ | |
> | Kiyana | | | | sometimes |

Section 4 Statement logic

Warm-up activity

1. Jeevan, Jasveer and Jasven explore the zoo together. Jeevan and Jasveer took photos of the tigers. Jeevan did not like the vultures but Jasven liked all the birds. Jasveer enjoyed feeding the penguins. Jeevan liked the elephants best.

	Jeevan	Jasveer	Jasven
tigers			
vultures			
elephants			
penguins			

   Now answer these questions.

   a) Does Jasven like penguins? ....

   b) Is it possible to say that any of the children definitely dislike tigers?

   ....

   c) Is there an animal which we can be sure Jasveer dislikes? ....

   d) How many of the children definitely like elephants? ....

2. Sally, Sarah, Stuart and Simon are all taking their CSEC exams. Stuart does not do any subject which involves art. His favourite subject is history. Simon and Sally are in all the same exams. Simon took nine CSEC subjects including biology but not history. Sally is taking art.

	Biology	History	Art
Sally			
Sarah			
Stuart			
Simon			

   a) We know nothing about which subjects one of the students is taking.

   What is this student's name? ....

   b) Did Sally take the CSEC history exam? ....

   c) Which two CSEC subjects is Simon definitely taking?

   ....

   d) Can we say for sure how many CSEC subjects Stuart is taking?

   ....

Statement logic

3 Leanne travels to dance club by bus.
James and his sister Lucy cycle to dance club.
Archie walks to dance club but is sometimes late.
James cycles faster than Lucy.

If the above statements are true, this must mean that only one of the following statements can be true. Circle the statement you believe must be true.

A Leanne's family have no car.

B James enjoys riding a bicycle.

C Only Leanne and Lucy like dance club.

D Sometimes Archie arrives at dance club on time.

4 Lawrence has four pet rabbits of different sizes.
Barty and Mollie are both black and white.
Flo is Barty's mother and the second largest rabbit.
Jim and Mollie are brother and sister.
Barty is the largest male rabbit, but smaller than his mother.

If the above statements are true, this must mean that only one of the following statements can be true. Which one? Circle the statement you believe must be true.

A Flo is the oldest rabbit.

B Mollie is the largest rabbit.

C Jim is Barty's father.

D Jim and Mollie are the same size.

Section 4 Statement logic

Just for fun

Developing logic skills – Word grid

Place the words into the blank grid so that each one can be read either across or down.

For example:

TOP	AWE
PEN	TEN
TAT	OWE

T	A	T
O	W	E
P	E	N

1 DRY ERR
ANY SUD
SEA URN

	E	
	R	
	R	

2 TEE ATE
ANT BOA
ONE BAT

A	T	E

3 EWE TWO
TOT SET
YET STY

	W	

4 EAT HEN
SPA ANT
SHE PEA

5 EGO HEW
DON AGO
WON HAD

6 EYE YOU
END EWE
NOW DUE

7 HAS SEW
ICE PEW
HIP ACE

8 TOE ANY
ONE TAB
EYE BEE

Challenge

Use a dictionary to find 6 three-letter words that work across and down. Fill in the grid but leave five blanks for your partner to complete.

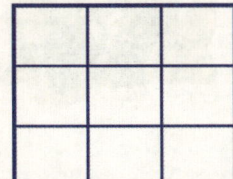

Worksheet 4a

Statement logic

Read the statements and then write your answer on the line provided.

For example:

Tom's house is due south of St Mary's Church and south-east of the village shop.

The village shop is due north of Taylor's Farm.

Taylor's Farm is south-west of St Mary's Church.

These four places form the points of a square.

Where is Tom's house in relation to Taylor's Farm?   _east_

1 Complete the correct compass directions on the following diagram, remembering to include not only the four main directions, but also those in between.

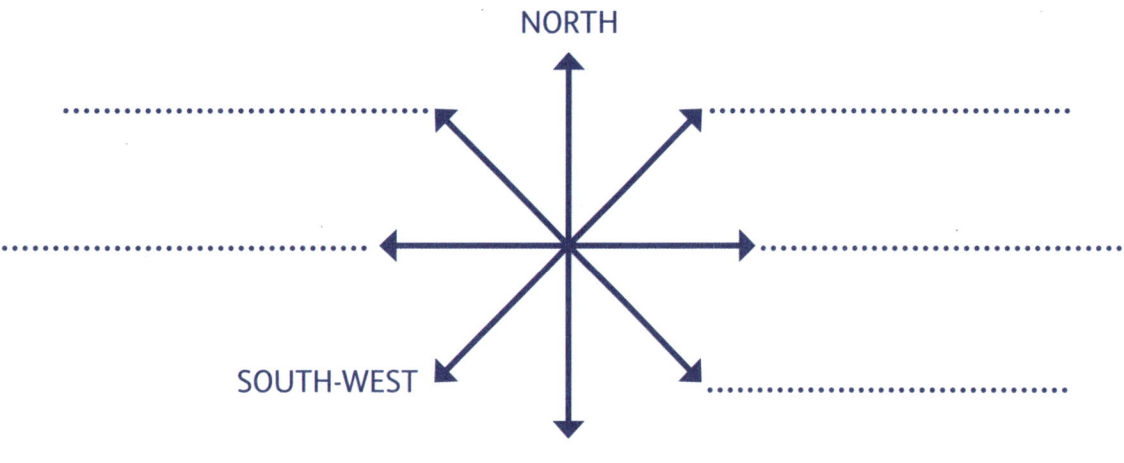

2 At a zoo, the monkey enclosure is due south of the insect house and south-west of the meerkats.

The penguins are due south of the meerkats.

The insect house is due west of the meerkats.

These four places form the points of a square.

Where is the insect house in relation to the penguins?

....

Section 4 Statement logic

3 Josh, Jess, Dan and Mia are on an outing to a theme park. ...../1

Josh and Mia love going on the fast rides.

Dan sits out the rollercoaster as it makes him sick.

Only Jess and Dan prefer the standard rides to the 3D rides.

Josh and Jess enjoy anything to do with ghosts!

Who is likely to enjoy the new high-speed 3D rollercoaster the most?

....

4 Daisy, Reece, Edward and Paige go to the same school and are all related. ...../1

Rachel is Daisy's mother and Paige's aunt.

Reece and Edward are brothers.

Anna is grandmother to all the children and has two daughters but no sons.

Paige has one brother and one sister.

What is the relationship between Daisy and Edward?

....

5 Avril, Samantha, Jiao and George all go to school on the same bus. ...../1

Samantha is three years older than Avril.

Avril is a year older than George.

Jiao and George are two years apart in age.

Jiao and Samantha are also two years apart in age.

How much older is Jiao than Avril?

....

Statement logic

6 Annie, Chris, Eusébio, Ed and Tim love sharing new games when they get together. ...../1

Tim has just downloaded the latest role-play game.

Annie and Eusébio like to play adventure games together.

Chris likes action games.

Ed and Eusébio are hooked on platform games.

Tim is Chris's best friend and they always download the same games.

Annie also enjoys puzzle games.

Who has the fewest kinds of game? ....

Record your score ...../11

Section 4 Statement logic

Worksheet 4b

Read each item, then answer the question that follows.

1 Lucy's mom makes sure she always serves a meal for Sunday lunch that the children will like.   ..../1

Lucy and her brother Jake both like cabbage.

Jake will not eat any other green vegetables but likes any kind of meat.

Lucy likes carrots and peas but will not eat chicken.

If the above statements are true, this must mean that only one of the following statements can be true. Which one? Circle the statement you believe must be true.

A Lucy's family only have roast meat on Sundays.

B Both children will eat cabbage and roast chicken.

C Mom never serves peas with Sunday lunch.

D The family sometimes have carrots and lamb.

2 Abi, Sam, Jiao and Lamar are at the pick and mix counter in the supermarket. They weigh their sweets to find out how much they have to pay.   ..../1

Abi's bag is the largest.

Jiao's bag is heavier than Lamar's.

Lamar has the fewest sweets.

Sam's bag is lighter than Jiao's but heavier than Lamar's.

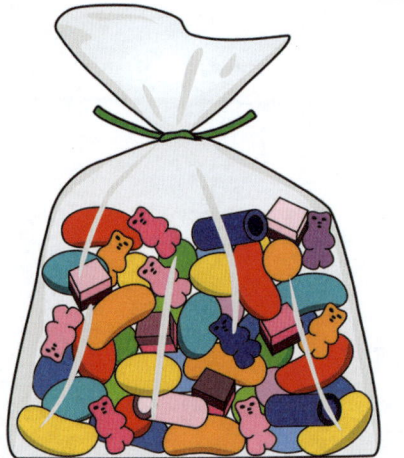

If the above statements are true, this must mean that only one of the following statements can be true. Circle the statement you believe must be true.

A Abi's sweets are the heaviest.

B Lamar's sweets are the lightest.

C Jiao has more sweets than Lamar.

D Sam has fewer sweets than Abi.

Statement logic

3 Barrie, Bethany, Ben, Betty and Boris meet every weekend to do a cycle ride. Betty arrives before Barrie but after Bethany. Ben passes Betty but is not the earliest to the meet. Boris wears a blue helmet and always arrives third.

..../1

If the above statements are true, this must mean that only one of the following statements can be true. Which one? Circle the statement you believe must be true.

A Ben arrives before everyone.

B Boris' favourite colour is blue.

C Betty and Barrie arrive at the same time.

D Bethany arrives first.

4 Jamie, Cavan, Megan, Ciara and Harry all receive weekly pocket money. Megan gets twice as much as Jamie but no more than Ciara. Cavan does lots of chores around the house. He gets his pocket money on a Friday. Cavan is the second best paid. Harry gets less than half of Megan's weekly amount. He keeps his in a piggybank in his bedroom. All the boys spend their money on a Friday in the local supermarket.

..../1

If the above statements are true, this must mean that only one of the following statements can be true. Which one? Circle the statement you believe must be true.

A Jamie has more pocket money than Harry.

B Harry puts his money into the bank.

C The girls spend their money on a Saturday.

D Cavan is saving for a new bike.

Section 4 Statement logic

5 Lisa, Emily, Catherine, Jemma and Katie are all related. Emily is not Jemma's sister but is always meeting up with Lisa. Katie has a sister but this is not Catherine. Lisa is a niece to Katie who is Jemma's mother. Emily and Katie are sisters. Lisa is one of the girls' siblings. Catherine is Katie's mum.

...../1

If the above statements are true, this must mean that only one of the following statements can be true. Which one? Circle the statement you believe must be true.

A Emily is Jemma's mother.

B Catherine is Jemma's grandmother.

C Catherine, Katie and Emily are sisters.

D Jemma and Lisa are sisters.

6 Ollie, Grace and Sam all walk to school and arrive together at nine o'clock. Ollie lives the furthest from the school and it takes him 30 minutes to walk to school. Grace takes 20 minutes to walk to school. Sam lives closer to the school so it only takes him 10 minutes to walk to school.

...../1

If the above statements are true, this must mean that only one of the following statements can be true. Which one? Circle the statement you believe must be true.

A Ollie leaves home to walk to school at 8:30 in the morning.

B Ollie is sometimes late for school.

C Sam walks twice as quickly as Grace.

D Ollie, Grace and Sam walk home from school together.

Record your score ...../6

32

Section 5: Essential part

> **Skills notes**
> - *Essential part:* to identify a component that the given noun or verb cannot function or exist without, not just something it might have.
>
> **For example:**
>
> Circle the word that is a necessary component of the word in bold.
>
> **Reggae**
>
> A Jamaica   B (music)
> C drums   D dance

Think it through

'Essential part' items challenge you to read through a list of words carefully to find one that is a necessary component of the keyword.

Answer choices will be included that distract you, but if you think logically of the link between the keyword in bold and each option in the list, you will be able to select the one that is its necessary component.

Working it out

In the example in the skills notes above, the keyword 'reggae' is linked in some way to all the words and phrases on the list.

Reggae	
	Reggae started in Jamaica, and is an important part of Jamaican culture, but reggae music can be played and created anywhere in the world.
	Reggae is a type of music. Without music, reggae cannot exist.
	Drums are commonly used in reggae, but not every reggae song must have drums. It's a key feature, but not essential.
	People often dance to reggae when they listen to it, but it is not essential.

Once you have selected the option that is linked to the keyword, complete this sentence in your head:

(Keyword) could not function or exist without (option). In this case, a *car* cannot function without an *engine*.

Section 5 Essential part

> **Tip**
>
> Focus on one word at a time and link it to the keyword.
>
> Put a ✗ or a ✓ next to each option as you work through their link to the keyword.

Warm-up activity

Think about each option for a table and write its Relationship. Then put a ✓ under Is essential or Not essential.

	Options	Relationship	Is essential	Not essential
table	a) vase			
	b) cloth			
	c) chair			
	d) legs			

Circle the option that is an essential component of the word in bold.

1 **research**   A hypothesis   B laboratory   C graphs   D respondents
2 **mountain**   A peak   B trail   C hikers   D stream
3 **library**   A chairs   B books   C students   D microfilm
4 **examination** A candidates   B centres   C pencils   D questions
5 **garden**   A bench   B shed   C flowers   D tools

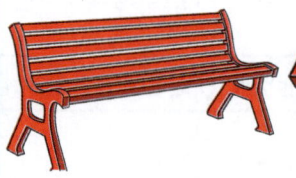

Essential part

Just for fun

Anagrams

Using the clues to help you, rearrange the letters to make a word.

For example:

CREUES   save from danger   RESCUE

1 **KLANWIG**   using your feet   ....
2 **SETORRE**   renovate something   ....
3 **SEPSRING**   exerting a force   ....
4 **ORACTR**   vegetable   ....
5 **TAMIAINN**   look after   ....
6 **NITREGCAR**   going back over   ....
7 **REHELAITH**   better for you   ....
8 **TIVSIQUIENI** always asking questions ....
9 **TRANIOLARI**   not using reason   ....

Challenge

1 Choose 3 to 5 interesting words from your reading book, spelling list or dictionary.
2 Scramble the letters of each word to create an anagram.
3 Write your own clue for each one.
4 Swap with a classmate and see if they can solve your puzzles.

_____
_____
_____
_____

Section 5 Essential part

Worksheet 5

Circle the option that is an essential component of the word in bold.

1 **bakery**   A donuts   B oven   ..../1
                  C coffee   D vanilla

2 **candle**   A wax   B fragrance   ..../1
                  C holder   D lighter

3 **bedroom**   A bed   B desk   ..../1
                  C closet   D window

4 **trip**   A aeroplane   B tickets   ..../1
                  C car   D destination

5 **gallery**   A receptionist B artist   ..../1
                  C art   D opening

6 **mall**   A elevator   B stores   ..../1
                  C shoppers   D security

7 **lake**   A boats   B water   ..../1
                  C divers   D jet skis

8 **farm**   A animals   B barns   ..../1
                  C tractor   D produce

9 **ice**   A freezer   B tray   ..../1
                  C water   D drink

10 **restaurant** A chairs   B servers   ..../1
                  C menu   D diners

Record your score ..../10

Worksheet 5

36

Section 6 — Words in a sequence

> **Skills notes**
> - *Word sequence:* to identify the pattern and select the word that comes next.
>
>   **For example:**
>
>   Select the word that comes next in the sequence.
>
>   accept, reject; build, demolish; win, lose; rise, ...
>
>   **A** (fall)   **B** raise   **C** risen   **D** climb

Finding the pattern

A pattern is a repeated arrangement. For this type of item, you will need to look at the first pair of words, determine their relationship to each other and decide if this relationship is repeated in the next pair.

Working it out

In the example in the skills notes above, look carefully at the words in the sequence to determine the part of speech; these are all verbs. Knowing this will help you to identify the relationship between them.

Next, look at the meaning of each word. This is another step in finding the relationship between the words and seeing if a pattern is established.

Let's deal with each pair.

Word	Meaning	Relationship
accept	to agree or allow	opposites
reject	to refuse or dismiss	
build	to construct something	opposites
demolish	to knock something down	
win	to achieve victory	opposites
lose	to fail to win	
rise	to move upwards	
?		

Section 6 Words in a sequence

Finally, look at the four options given to find the verb that is the opposite of the incomplete pair.

Tip

Some patterns to look out for include synonyms and antonyms, tenses and changing word forms, for example, verb to noun or noun to adjective.

Warm-up activity

Write the antonym of the following words.

1 genuine ....
2 delight ....
3 cowardice ....
4 clumsy ....
5 ignorance ....

Write the synonym of the following words.

6 approach ....
7 dangerous ....
8 contrast ....
9 impartial ....
10 distinguished ....

Form nouns from the given words.

11 try ....

12 collide ....

13 discover ....

Form adjectives from the given words.

14 continue ....

15 create ....

16 luck ....

Section 6 Words in a sequence

Just for fun

Deductive reasoning

Read the statements and answer the questions. Use the space below the questions for working out.

> **For example:**
>
> In four years' time, my grandmother will be exactly five times as old as I am now.
>
> My grandmother is now 56. How old am I?   <u>12</u>

1 A is faster than B and C. C is faster than B. Who is slowest? ....

2 Y is hotter than X or Z. Z is cooler than X. Which is the coolest? ....

3 Ben is five years older than Tom. Kim is three years younger than Ben.
   Who is the oldest? ....

4 Nicholas is 15 years younger than his brother Will, and four years older than his brother Richie. Their dad is ten times as old as Richie and five times as old as Nicholas.

   How old is Will? ....

Just for fun

40

Words in a sequence

5 Dale jumps 1.20 m, 4 cm higher than Jack, and Jodi jumps higher than Jack. Chris jumps 3 cm less than Jack and 7 cm less than Jodi.

How high did Jodi jump? ....

6 Lucy scores 80% in a maths test. Kylie gets 15 marks, which is 20% less than Lucy and Molly gets 3 marks less than Lucy. How many marks did the three girls gain all together? ....

7 Trains leave the station every 45 minutes, with the first train each day leaving at 8:45 a.m. The bus from Tom's house to the station takes 25 minutes. If there is a bus every 20 minutes starting from 8 a.m., at what time must he get the bus to arrive 10 minutes before the third train of the day? ....

41

Section 6 Words in a sequence

8 Fay is four times as old as her little sister and a third of her mother's age. If her mother is 40 in four years' time, how old is Fay's little sister now? ....

9 Carrie is 50 cm taller than Sal and 40 cm shorter than Bella. Tia is 10 cm taller than Carrie. Bella is the tallest. If Carrie is 120 cm tall, who is the shortest person and how tall are they? ....

Challenge

Write your own deductive reasoning problem for a classmate to solve.

1. Write three short statements using clues that compare people, times, ages or measurements.
2. End with a clear question for your classmate to work out.
3. Use logical steps so that your puzzle has only one correct answer.
4. Include space for your solver to work out the answer.

Statement 1: _____

Statement 2: _____

Statement 3: _____

Question: _____

Answer: _____

Worksheet 6

Circle the word that completes the sequence.

1. commerce, commercial; tragedy, tragic; miracle, miraculous; question, … ...../1
   - A questions
   - B questioned
   - C questionable
   - D questioning

2. fly, soar; hate, loathe; funny, humorous; fair, … ...../1
   - A unbiased
   - B indifferent
   - C partial
   - D selective

3. accident, accidental; artist, artistic; fame, … ...../1
   - A famously
   - B infamous
   - C famed
   - D famous

4. ally, enemy; broad, narrow; calm, furious; conceal, … ...../1
   - A hidden
   - B divulge
   - C shrouding
   - D saving

5. keep, maintain; necessary, critical; accrue, … ...../1
   - A accrual
   - B accumulate
   - C need
   - D perceive

6. announce, announcement; omit, omission; complain, … ...../1
   - A complained
   - B complains
   - C complaining
   - D complaint

7. wind, windy; rust, rustic; nature, … ...../1
   - A unnatural
   - B unnaturally
   - C natural
   - D naturally

8. tasty, delectable; keen, fervent; idea, … ...../1
   - A concept
   - B conception
   - C conceptual
   - D conceptually

Section 6 Words in a sequence

9 clarify, explain; risky, perilous; definitive, … ..../1
  A decision B decisive
  C decided D decides

10 predicament, dilemma; accurate, precise; recount, … ..../1
  A narrated B narrator
  C narrating D narrate

Record your score ..../10

Section 7 Number sequences

> **Skills notes**
> - *Number sequence:* to identify the missing number(s) from a number sequence.
>
> **For example:**
>
> Select the number that completes the sequence.
>
> 7, 14, 21, 28, 35, ...
>
> **A** 39   **B** (42)   **C** 49   **D** 56

Look for the pattern

A number sequence uses addition, subtraction, multiplication or division (and occasionally two of these operations) to build a series of numbers in a row.

As the name suggests, these questions are all about numbers 'in sequence', which means they fit a certain pattern.

The calculations generally work with small number steps. Here are some examples of what you might see:

- a simple sequence with only one rule such as adding the same number, or even an extra number, for example, +1, +2, +3, each time

- a sequence that works for alternate (or even every three) numbers, for example, numbers 1, 3 and 5 follow a different pattern to 2, 4 and 6

- a two-step sequence where you need to make two calculations, for example, ×2 +1 to get to the next number

- alternate sequences that relate to each other, for example, the first, third and fifth numbers could be multiplied by 2, and the second, fourth and sixth numbers could be multiplied by 3.

Section 7 Number sequences

Working it out

Simple sequences

Using the example in the skills notes on the previous page, first take a look at the pattern of numbers: if they look quite evenly spaced they may follow a simple sequence.

    7, 14, 21, 28, 35, ...

The spacing looks quite even so look at the first two numbers. How did you get from the first to the second?

    7, 14   Add 7 to make 14.

Then look at the next numbers in the sequence. Do you do the same?

    14, 21   Add another 7 to make 21.

Yes, so the pattern in this number sequence is 'add 7 each time'.

    7, 14, 21, 28, 35, 42

> **Tip**
>
> Sometimes the gap between all the numbers seems different every time. This may be because the operation being used is: 'add next multiple of the same number each time', moving up the times table, for example:
>
>   using the 4 times table, add 4, add 8, add 12, add 16, and so on.

Alternate sequences

Alternate sequences are often easy to spot because the numbers are not evenly spaced, or the pattern may appear to be random:

    5, 16, 6, 14, 7, 12

In this sequence the first, third and fifth numbers are much smaller than the second, fourth and sixth, so there are two rules or patterns in action:

    5, 16, 6, 14, 7, 12   Add 1 for every alternate number.

    5, 16, 6, 14, 7, 12   Subtract 2 for the other alternate numbers.

So here the number sequence is juggling two separate operations (adding 1 / subtracting 2) at the same time.

Number sequences

If there do not appear to be enough numbers to work out a sequence, look to see if there is a relationship between the two number sequences:

   3, 12, 6, 24, 10, ...

The first and third numbers are multiplied by 4 to give the number that follows. So, multiply 10 by 4 and you will have reached the answer:

   3, 12, 6, 24, 10, 40

> **Tip**
>
> If you are asked for the first number in a sequence, remember to reverse the rule, for example: ...., 6, 9, 12. The rule is to add 3, so subtract 3 to get to the answer!

Warm-up activity 1

Read each item carefully.

1. This number sequence has no numbers missing from it. But can you work out the rule behind this sequence? What is going on here? Write a short explanation of the rule below.

   | 1 | 2 | 4 | 8 | 16 | 32 | 64 |

   ....

   ....

Select the number that completes the sequence.

2. 12, 15, 18, 21, 24, …

   A 24   B 25   C 26   D 27

3. 11, 22, 15, 19, 19, 16, …

   A 14   B 22   C 23   D 32

Section 7 Number sequences

For items 4 to 6, write the missing numbers in the spaces provided in the sequence.

4   8, 16, ..., 32, 40, ...

5   16, 20, 14, 40, 12, ..., ...

6   ...., 7, 15, ..., 43, 63

Warm-up activity 2

A good way to start these questions is by working out the gap between a number and the number next to it. You might want to write this above the two numbers, like this:

2, $^{+2}$ 4, $^{+2}$ 6,

Practise the skill with these examples, adding the pattern above the numbers.

1   9, 18, 27, 36, 45   ....

2   13, 26, 39, 52, 65   ....

3   2, 4, 8, 16, 32   ....

4   64, 56, 48, 40, 32   ....

Sometimes there will be two different patterns at work in the sequence. See if you can identify what is happening in these questions. Record the gaps between the numbers again, but this time compare the first, third and fifth numbers, and then the second, fourth and sixth numbers.

5   38, 45, 42, 49, 46, 53   ....

6   13, 26, 26, 36, 52, 46   ....

7   67, 62, 64, 59, 61, 56   ....

8   37, 41, 43, 35, 49 29   ....

9   12, 27, 24, 9, 48, 3   ....

Number sequences

Other questions of this type involve squared or cubed numbers, or adding previous numbers together to give the next number. Work out the rule for these sequences, and write it on the line provided.

10 7, 8, 15, 23, 38, 61 ....

11 14, 15, 29, 44, 73 ....

12 81, 64, 49, 36, 25, 16 ....

13 289, 324, 361, 400, 441 ....

14 8, 27, 64, 125, 216 ....

Section 7 Number sequences

Just for fun

Number patterns

Find five different patterns using this number square grid. Use different colours to mark the patterns you find. Then use the patterns to write your own questions. One pattern is marked for you, in bold.

1	2	**3**	4	5	**6**	7	8	**9**	10
11	**12**	13	14	**15**	16	17	**18**	19	20
21	22	23	24	25	26	27	28	29	30
31	32	33	34	35	36	37	38	39	40
41	42	43	44	45	46	47	48	49	50
51	52	53	54	55	56	57	58	59	60
61	62	63	64	65	66	67	68	69	70
71	72	73	74	75	76	77	78	79	80
81	82	83	84	85	86	87	88	89	90
91	92	93	94	95	96	97	98	99	100

1 ....
2 ....
3 ....
4 ....
5 ....

Challenge

Look at the patterns you found. Choose one and write a riddle or clue to describe it without showing the numbers. Can a classmate work out which pattern you used?

Worksheet 7

Circle the number that completes each number sequence.

1 9, 12, 15, 18, 21, …
   A 22   **B** 24   **C** 28   **D** 32   ...../1

2 4, 8, 16, 32, 64, …
   A 72   **B** 96   **C** 116   **D** 128   ...../1

3 1, 2, 4, 7, 11, 16, …
   A 22   **B** 24   **C** 26   **D** 28   ...../1

4 2, 6, 18, 54, …
   A 162   **B** 108   **C** 216   **D** 218   ...../1

5 91, 97, 101, 107, 111, …
   A 123   **B** 121   **C** 117   **D** 115   ...../1

6 16, 4, 24, 6, 32, …
   A 10   **B** 8   **C** 64   **D** 48   ...../1

7 23, 24, 26, 29, 33, 38, 44, …
   A 49   **B** 51   **C** 54   **D** 56   ...../1

8 3, 3, 6, 18, 72, …
   A 160   **B** 224   **C** 360   **D** 418   ...../1

9 8, 9, 17, 26, 43, 69, …
   A 112   **B** 103   **C** 95   **D** 86   ...../1

10 27, 64, 125, 216, …
   A 289   **B** 324   **C** 343   **D** 361   ...../1

Record your score ...../10

Section 8 Number analogies

> **Skills notes**
>
> - *Number analogy:* to find the missing number by identifying a rule and applying it.
>
> **For example:**
>
> The first two pairs of numbers are related in the same way. Establish the relationship between these pairs and complete the last pair in the same way.
>
> (7 is to 49)   (8 is to 64)   (6 is to …)
>
> **A** 60   **B** 30   **C** 36   **D** 24

Finding the relationship

Two numbers per group

Just as you worked out the analogies (or relationships) between words previously, you are using your powers of deduction to work out the relationships between numbers here.

You will be given groups of numbers, all of which follow the same rule. For example, if the rule in the first group is to double the first number to get to the second number (4 is to 8), the second group will show a different pair of numbers that follow the same rule (3 is to 6).

Once you have worked out the common rule, you just need to do the same to the incomplete group to reach the answer.

Working it out

In the example in the skills notes above, begin by looking at the size of the numbers in the first set of brackets. If the numbers are close together, there is possibly an addition or subtraction sum involved. If they are further apart, there may be a multiplication or division calculation involved.

Number analogies

(7 is to 49)

These numbers are quite far apart so think about your times tables.

(7 is to 49)   7 × 7 = 49

You should recognise 49 as 7 × 7 or 7^2 (seven squared – the number multiplied by itself). Next, look at the second set of brackets. The number will either be multiplied by 7 or by itself.

(8 is to 64)   8 × 8 = 64

Now that you know the calculation is a square number, do the same to the third set of brackets.

(6 is to 36)   because 6 × 6 = 36

Three numbers per group

Another type of number analogy you might see has three numbers rather than two per group. This is a two-step question, which is slightly more difficult.

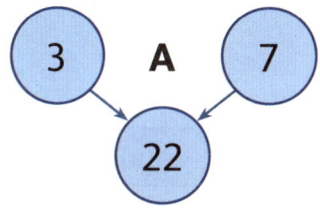 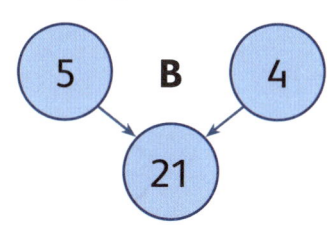 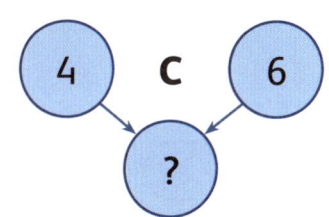

Begin again with the first group. This time, look at the upper numbers. Is there a large or small gap between the numbers?

(3 [22] 7)   3 × 7 = 21   3 + 7 = 10

This looks like a multiplication sum, but 3 × 7 is 21, not 22. This suggests there may be two steps to the calculation. Think about what you would have to do to get to the answer.

(3 [22] 7)   3 × 7 = 21   21 + 1 = 22

Adding 1 to the multiplication gives the right answer. Now see if this works with the next group.

(5 [21] 4)   5 × 4 = 20   20 + 1 = 21

The rule is to multiply the numbers together and add 1, so you can answer the question.

(4 [25] 6)   because 4 × 6 = 24   24 + 1 = 25

53

Section 8 Number analogies

> **Tip**
>
> Draw on the same skills you use for identifying the rules in sequences for number analogies.
>
> Number analogies may be presented in several ways, so it is important to focus on identifying the patterns and rules and applying them to find the missing number.

Warm-up activity 1

1. Connect each group, P, Q, R, S, to the correct operation in the lozenges below, by working out how to reach the number in the top left circle.

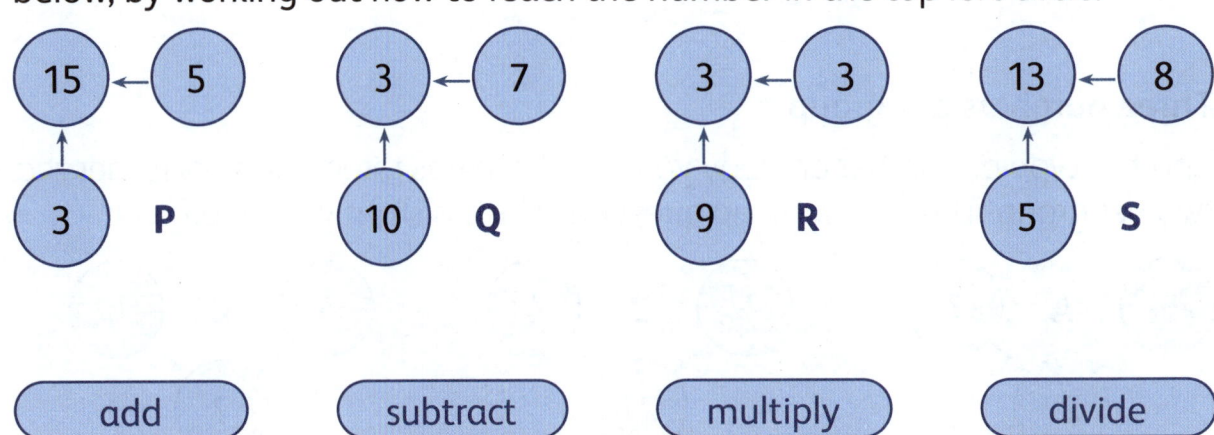

(add) (subtract) (multiply) (divide)

For items 2 and 3, the first two pairs of numbers are related in the same way. Establish the relationship between these pairs and complete the last pair in the same way. Circle the letter beneath the correct answer.

2. (9 is to 19)
   (5 is to 15)
   (7 is to …)

   A 9   B 27   C 3   D 17

Number analogies

3 (11 is to 24)
(7 is to 16)
(4 is to ...)

A 8   **B** 10   **C** 12   **D** 13

For items 4 to 6, the three numbers in each set of brackets are all related in the same way. Work out how they are related, from the first two sets of brackets, then apply the same pattern to complete the third set. Write the missing numbers on the lines provided.

4 (15 [11] 4)   (22 [14] 8)   (9 [........] 6)

5 (12 [6] 3)   (20 [7] 4)   (28 [........] 7)

6 (12 [9] 6)   (21 [18] 15)   (15 [........] 9)

55

Section 8 Number analogies

Warm-up activity 2

Read the instructions for each section carefully.

This question type involves finding relationships between numbers. The numbers in both pairs are related to each other in the same way. Write the relationship between the two pairs of numbers.

With these simpler questions, you only need to decide whether the numbers have been added, subtracted, multiplied or divided.

1 (56 is to 7)   (32 is to 4)   ....
2 (29 is to 16)   (35 is to 22)   ....
3 (72 is to 101)   (63 is to 92)   ....
4 (96 is to 8)   (60 is to 5)   ....
5 (70 is to 35)   (59 is to 24)   ....
6 (14 is to 48)   (53 is to 87)   ....

Trickier questions of this type may involve squared or cubed numbers, triangular numbers or square roots. In other questions you may need to take two steps to solve the problem. Write the relationship between the two pairs of numbers.

7   (9 is to 86)   (11 is to 106)   ....
8   (11 is to 121) (12 is to 144)   ....
9   (15 is to 32)   (17 is to 36)   ....
10 (9 is to 82)   (6 is to 37)   ....
11 (13 is to 42)   (14 is to 45)   ....
12 (1 is to 3)   (6 is to 10)   ....
13 (2 is to 8)   (5 is to 125)   ....
14 (2 is to 3)   (5 is to 7)   ....

Number analogies

Just for fun

Translating and combining images

Look at the picture on the left. One of the white shapes on the right is an exact match. Circle the letter under the shape that matches exactly.

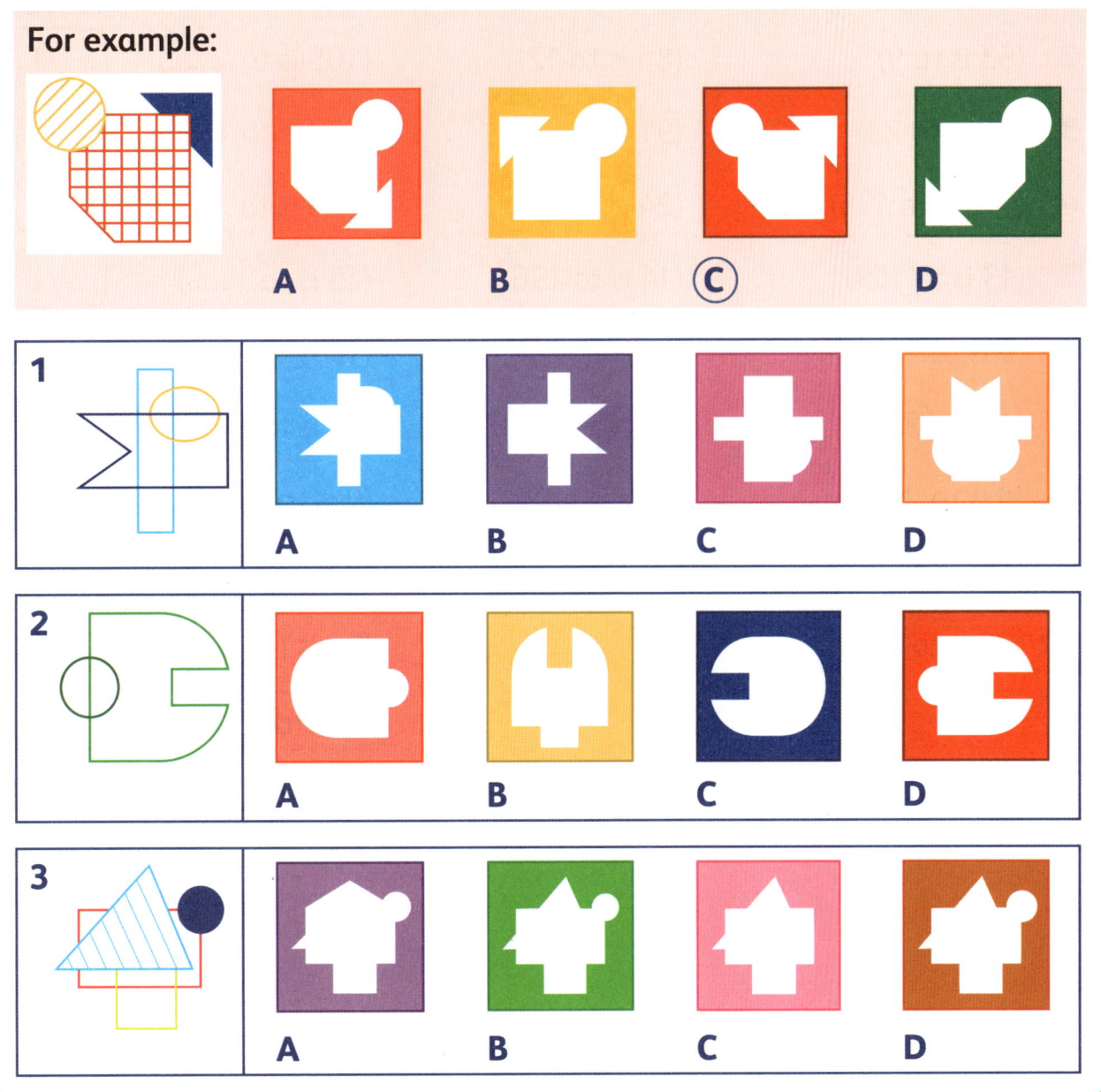

Challenge

Create your own pattern with at least five elements. Then, make three 'wrong' continuations and one correct one. See if your partner can find the match.

Section 8 Number analogies

Worksheet 8

The first two pairs of numbers are related in the same way. Establish the relationship between these pairs and complete the last pair in the same way. Write the answer on the line provided.

1 (15 is to 45)   (16 is to 48)   (17 is to ....)   ...../1
2 (63 is to 9)   (84 is to 12)   (105 is to ....)   ...../1
3 (75 is to 23)   (91 is to 39)   (107 is to ....)   ...../1
4 (119 is to 135)   (247 is to 263)   (369 is to ....)   ...../1
5 (13 is to 169)   (14 is to 196)   (15 is to ....)   ...../1
6 (9 is to 22)   (11 is to 26)   (13 is to ....)   ...../1
7 (4 is to 27)   (9 is to 52)   (11 is to ....)   ...../1
8 (3 is to 20)   (7 is to 48)   (9 is to ....)   ...../1
9 (125 is to 216)   (343 is to 512)   (729 is to ....)   ...../1
10 (29 is to 31)   (37 is to 41)   (53 is to ....)   ...../1

Record your score ...../10

Maths workout 1

Place value

Write the answers on the lines provided.

1. What is the value of the underlined digit in each number?

   a) 13<u>5</u>0   ....

   b) 1<u>0</u>34750   ....

   c) 15.<u>5</u>6   ....

   d) 2.7<u>8</u>   ....

2. Write these numbers in ascending order.

   1967   1976   1769   1796

   ....

3. Write these numbers in descending order.

   40   45   65

   ....

4. The value of the 9 in 4967 is 900 (9 hundreds).

   a) What is the value of the 3 in 143 675? ....

   b) In the number 46 016, how many times greater is the value of the 6 on the left than the 6 on the right? ....

5. Rewrite each of these numbers with a decimal point so that the 8 in each number has a value of 8 tenths.

   a) 438   ....

   b) 7981   ....

   c) 85   ....

6. Write these numbers in order of decreasing size.

   3.45   4.53   3.54   5.34   4.35

   ....

Maths workout 2

Finding the original amount

Write your answers on the lines provided. Use the space below each item for working out.

1 If $\frac{1}{2}$ of the total amount is 4, what is the total amount?   ....

2 If $\frac{1}{3}$ of the total amount is 12, what is the total amount?   ....

3 If $\frac{1}{7}$ of the whole is 10, what is the whole?   ....

4 If $\frac{2}{3}$ of a number is 18, what is the number?   ....

5 If $\frac{3}{7}$ of a number is 27, what is the number?   ....

6 If $\frac{5}{12}$ of a number is 60, what is the number? ....

7 When a number is divided by 3, the result is 11.
What is the number? ....

8 When a number is divided by 10, the result is 18.
What is the number? ....

9 If $\frac{5}{9}$ of a number is 45, what is the original number? ....

Maths workout 3

Formulae

Write your answers on the lines provided.

1. Peter thought of a number. When he subtracts 5 from his number, the result is 7. What number did Peter think of? ....

2. Write each word sentence as a formula.

   a) Subtract 5 from x ....

   b) Multiply y by 10 ....

3. a) How many centimetres are there in a metre? ....

   b) How many centimetres are there in:

   i. 5 metres ....

ii. 9 metres? ....

c) Write a formula for the number of centimetres in *n* metres.

....

4 Sophie thought of a number. She added 4, then multiplied the result by 3.

a) Write an expression to represent her final result.

....

b) If Sophie thought of the number 6, what was her final result?

....

Maths workout 4

Venn diagrams

Write your answers on the lines provided.

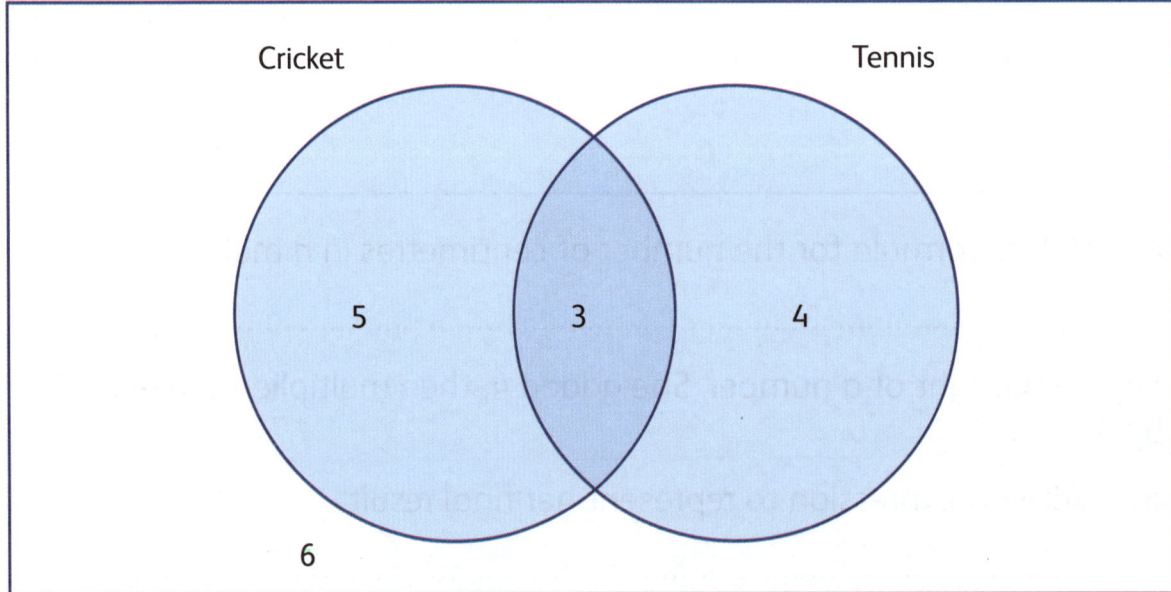

This Venn diagram shows the number of boys in a class who play cricket and tennis in the summer term.

a) How many boys play tennis but not cricket?

....

b) How many boys play neither tennis nor cricket?

....

c) How many boys are in the class?

....

About the practice papers

In this section, you will find four complete Ability Test practice papers. Use them as part of your preparation for your Ability Test exam.

Most of the items are similar to the ones you will see on your exam paper. This is to increase your level of comfort with the PEP exams in general. All the items will improve your reasoning and critical thinking skills.

Here are some things to remember for each practice paper:

- There are 40 items.
- You have 1 hour 15 minutes to answer all the items. This is the same time allotted for the real exam.
- Read each instruction and item carefully.
- Circle the letter of the answer you select. Under exam conditions, you will shade the letter (A, B, C, D) that corresponds to the answer you have selected for each item.
- Each item is worth 1 mark. When you, your peer or your teacher is marking the practice paper, if your answer is correct, 1 mark should be noted in the box to the right of each item. Tally your score at the end of each practice paper.

Practice paper 1

General instructions

There are 40 items in this practice paper. Read each item carefully, then circle the letter with the correct answer. There is only one correct answer for each item.

For items 1 to 3, select the word that best completes the statement.

1 Ruler is to length as scales are to … . ...../1

    A weight

    B heavy

    C measure

    D gauge

2 Late is to time as far is to … . ...../1

    A lost

    B away

    C distance

    D map

3 Entrance is to in as exit is to … . ...../1

    A emergency

    B out

    C leave

    D door

Practice paper 1

In items 4 and 5, which word does not belong in the group?

4 A elbow

   B thumb

   C knuckle

   D finger

5 A rain

   B snow

   C hail

   D winter

For items 6 and 7, select the most appropriate pair of words to complete each sentence.

6 Profits … but staff … declined.

   A peaked; moral

   B piqued; moral

   C peaked; morale

   D piqued; morale

7 Carl said he … the noise but refused to be … by it.

   A heard; detracted

   B heard; distracted

   C herd; detracted

   D herd; distracted

Practice paper 1

Each group below has words that are alike in some way.
Use them to answer items 8 and 9.

8 | duplicate   same   twin   equal |

Which of the following is NOT like the words in the group above?

A different

B similar

C identical

D equivalent

9 | apartment   house   condo   mansion |

Which of the following is NOT like the words in the group above?

A chalet

B castle

C office

D villa

Read the passage below carefully, then use it to answer item 10 below.

> Mike, Michael, Mark and Morris did a spelling test. Mark scored more than Michael but less than Mike. The test had twenty words and Morris was the only one who scored in the 'teens'. Mike correctly spelled double the score Michael achieved. Michael was pleased with half marks.

10 If the above statements are true, this must mean that only one of the following statements can be true. Which one? Circle the statement you believe must be true.

A Mark scored more than Morris in the spelling test.

B Mike answered all the spellings correctly.

C Michael did not come last in the test.

D Morris and Mark have the same score.

Practice paper 1

For items 11 to 13, circle the option that is an essential element of the word in bold.

11 ceremony
- A graduation
- B musician
- C seating
- D programme

...../1

12 investigation
- A purpose
- B suspects
- C results
- D crime

...../1

13 tennis
- A trophy
- B spectators
- C concessionaire
- D opponents

...../1

For items 14 and 15, select the word that comes next in the sequence.

14 develop, development; elect, election; distribute, distribution; betray, ….

- A betrayed
- B betrayal
- C betrays
- D betraying

...../1

15 child, childish; laugh, …; hate, hateful; amuse, amusing

- A laughing
- B laughter
- C laughable
- D laughed

...../1

69

Practice paper 1

Read the passage below carefully, then answer items 16 to 19.

Black River

Black River has changed over the years. It went from a bustling, thriving township to one that is known for its slow pace and a relaxed atmosphere.

In the late nineteenth century, Black River was one of Jamaica's flourishing townships. Its economic activity and prosperity were supported by its seaport, coupled with a strong manufacturing industry based on raw materials such as logwood and bamboo. Both were valuable exports to England and Europe; logwood, because the colour extracted from it was used to dye textiles, and bamboo because of the paper made from it by the Lacovia Manufacturing Company in St. Elizabeth.

Black River was also the scene of several first-time events in Jamaica's history. The very first telephone in the country was installed there in 1883, only seven years after Alexander Graham Bell first used his invention. Black River was the first Jamaican town with electricity in 1893, a mere 13 years after Thomas Edison patented the light bulb. In 1903, the first car in Jamaica arrived via the seaport in Black River.

Owing to some setbacks, Black River has seen a reduction in its commercial atmosphere and has not regained the prominence it once had. There was a fire in the early twentieth century, which destroyed half of the town. The closure of the port in 1968 further slowed the economic activity of the town.

16 The sentence 'It went from a bustling, thriving township to one that is known for its slow pace and a relaxed atmosphere' shows a …

    A comparison between Black River's past and the present.

    B comparison between Black River and other townships.

    C contrast between Black River's past and the present.

    D contrast between Black River and other townships.

17 Which of the following is true according to paragraph two? ...../1

   A Black River only thrived because the residents farmed logwood and bamboo.

   B Dye extraction from logwood was one of the main economic activities in Black River.

   C The Lacovia Manufacturing Company produced paper from bamboo in Black River.

   D Both the seaport and manufacturing activities contributed to the town's economy.

18 Why is the phrase 'only seven years after Alexander Graham Bell first used his invention' used in paragraph three? ...../1

   A to show how quickly Black River adopted the new technology

   B to prove that Alexander Graham Bell supported the town's economy

   C to show that telephones were installed in Black River before electricity

   D to prove that the people from Black River were competitive

19 Which of the following words has the same meaning as 'setback' used in the passage? ...../1

   A misfortune
   B achievement
   C impact
   D encounter

Practice paper 1

Read the passage below carefully, then use it to answer item 20.

> Raina has been given five gifts for her birthday. Gift A has red wrapping paper and a yellow bow. Gift B has blue wrapping paper. Gift C and Gift D both have spotty wrapping paper and no bows. Gift E has both a tag and bow. All of the gifts except Gift A have a gift tag. Gift B is wrapped in the same paper as Gift C. One gift has a birthday card attached.

20 If the statements above are true, this must mean that only one of the following statements can be true. Which one?
Circle the statement you believe must be true.   ....../1

    A Two gifts have red wrapping paper.

    B Only gifts with spotty paper have no bows.

    C Gift E has a yellow bow.

    D Three gifts have spotty wrapping paper.

For item 21, select the number that completes the sequence.

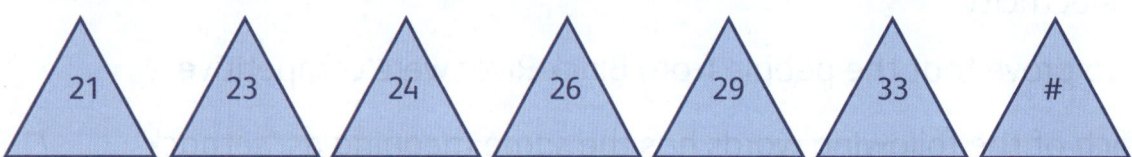

21 Which number correctly replaces #?   ....../1

    A 40

    B 38

    C 35

    D 37

Examine the pattern below. Use it to answer item 22.

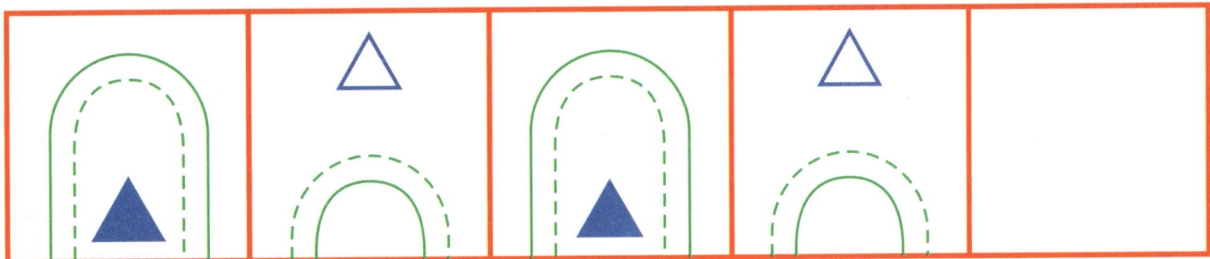

22 Circle the answer that comes next in the pattern.

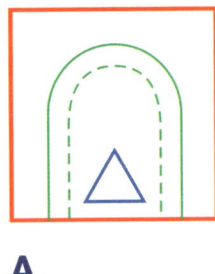 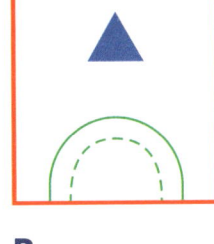 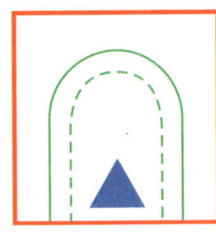 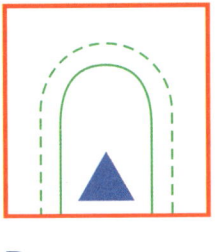

A   **B**   **C**   **D**

Look at the three groups labelled, L, M, N. Establish the relationship in group L. The same operation is used in group M and group N. Use the operation to find the missing number in group N in item 23.

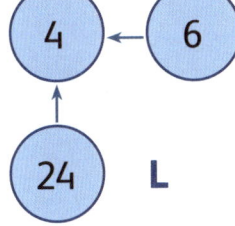   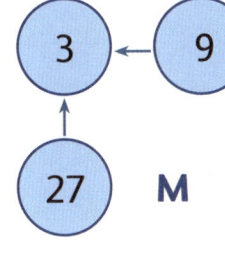   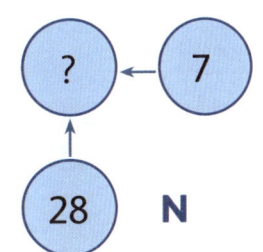

23 L (24 [4] 6)
   M (27 [3] 9)
   N (28 [?] 7)

   A 21

   B 4

   C 35

   D 3

Practice paper 1

24 What is the smallest number that can be added to 99 so that it can be divided by both 3 and 5? ...../1

A 3

B 4

C 5

D 6

25 Clare, Gemma, Tammy and Jackie are running a race. Clare crosses the finish line in 156 seconds. Gemma finishes 22 seconds after Clare. Tammy crosses the finish line 7 seconds ahead of Gemma, while Jackie finishes 26 seconds before Gemma. ...../1

Select the medal podium which shows who placed first, second and third in the race.

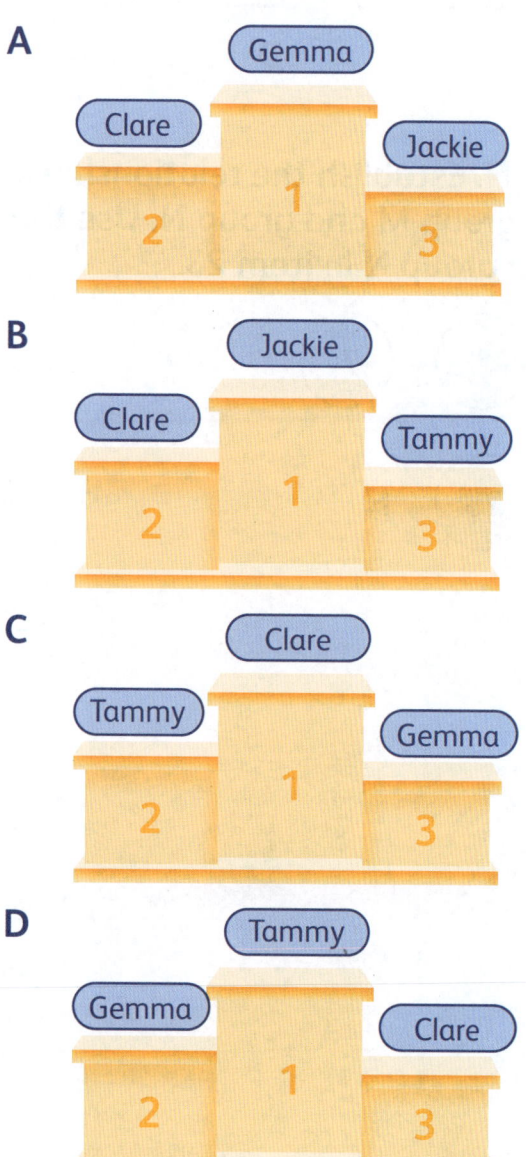

74

26 If I multiply a number by 4, I get the same answer when I triple it and add 9. Select the equation which will correctly solve for the original number.   ..../1

  A 4x = 3x + 9

  B 4x = 3x − 9

  C 3x = 4x + 9

  D 3x = 4x − 9

27 Barkley gets home from school 15 minutes later than his usual time. He played video games for half an hour, then takes 5 minutes to change before walking 10 minutes to his football club. He is at the football club for 1 hour and 40 minutes before returning home at 6:05 p.m. What time does Barkley usually get home from school?   ..../1

  A 3:20 p.m.

  B 3:15 p.m.

  C 3:10 p.m.

  D 3:00 p.m.

28 When Shanoya got to summer camp she realised she forgot the three-digit code to the lock on her suitcase. Her father sends her the following text: ..../1

  • The number is between 135 and 170.
  • The code is a multiple of 6.
  • The digits in the code add up to less than 9.

What is Shanoya's code?

  A 144

  B 150

  C 156

  D 162

29 Estimate the number of circles in the rectangle.
Do not count them.

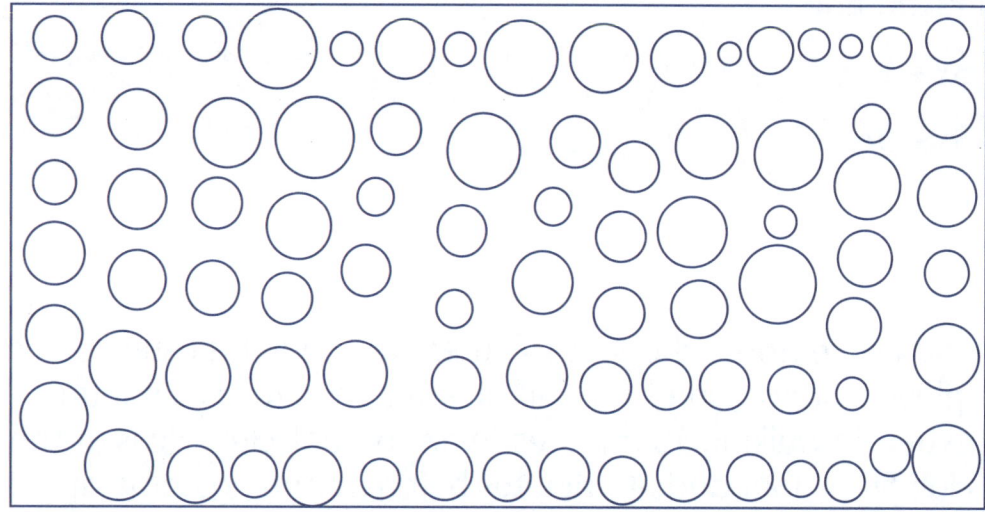

A 50

B 90

C 160

D 130

30 Jane worked for 7 hours delivering flyers and her friend Sarah
worked for 1 hour. In total they are paid $24,000. How much
does Sarah get paid?

A $3 000

B $1 000

C $6 000

D $21,000

31 Which fraction is equivalent to $\frac{6}{20}$?

A $\frac{3}{5}$

B $\frac{5}{9}$

C $\frac{2}{10}$

D $\frac{5}{10}$

32 The length of this rectangle is twice its width. What is the perimeter of the rectangle? ..../1

120 cm

Not drawn accurately

- **A** 240 cm
- **B** 260 cm
- **C** 360 cm
- **D** 380 cm

33 Peter, Alex and Michelle share sweets in a bag in the ratio 4 : 3 : 2. ..../1
Michelle receives 8 sweets. How many sweets does Peter receive?

- **A** 8
- **B** 9
- **C** 12
- **D** 16

Practice paper 1

34 Below is an overhead view of Rebecca's bedroom. ...../1

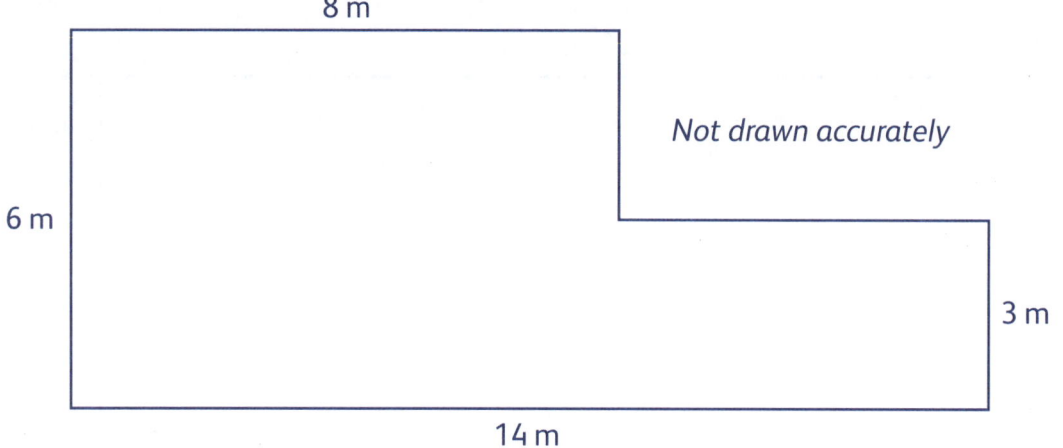

Carpet costs $840 per square metre. How much will it cost to carpet Rebecca's bedroom?

A $58,260

B $56,060

C $55,050

D $55,440

35 Which one of these events will certainly happen? ...../1

A I will get something wrong tomorrow.

B My brother's favourite team will win soon.

C Tuesday will follow Monday.

D The total of two spinners will be 13.

36 What number is marked by the arrow on the scale below? ...../1

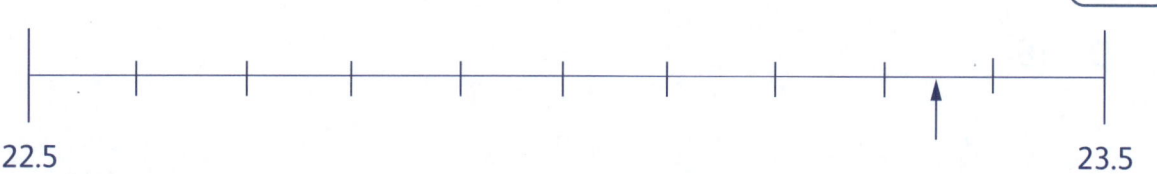

22.5   23.5

A 23.3

B 23.35

C 23.45

D 22.9

37 Which of these statements is correct? ...../1

A $9.6 > 9\frac{3}{5}$

B $9.6 < 9\frac{1}{2}$

C $9.6 = 9\frac{1}{2}$

D $9.6 = 9\frac{3}{5}$

38 The two-way table shows the colours and varieties of flowers in Sophia's bouquet. ...../1

	Roses	Tulips
Red	9	10
Yellow	6	7
Orange	7	5

Without looking, Sophia picks one flower to give to her mum. Which of the following statements is true?

A Picking a red rose is more likely than picking a red tulip.

B Picking an orange flower is more likely than picking a yellow flower.

C Picking a rose and a tulip are equally likely.

D Picking a red rose is less likely than picking a yellow rose.

39 A class has x boys and y girls. There are 5 more boys than girls. What is the value of y? ...../1

A $y = 5x$

B $y = x + 5$

C $y = x - 5$

D $y = x$

Practice paper 1

40 Below is part of the bus timetable for the route from Marton to Hopesfield.

..../1

Marton	06:10	07:15	07:40	07:50	08:15
Rickington	06:35	07:43	08:11	08:15	08:45
Barton	06:49	08:01	–	08:37	09:10
Brilliton	06:58	08:14	–	08:55	09:30
Chapplesmith	07:13	08:32	–	09:16	09:55
Hopesfield	07:26	08:49	08:59	09:35	10:15

It takes 5 minutes to walk from the bus stop to the town centre in Hopesfield. At what time should Tanya catch the bus from Marton if she wants to be in Hopesfield Town Centre at 9 o'clock?

A 06:10

B 07:15

C 07:40

D 07:50

Record your score ..../40

Practice paper 2

General instructions

There are 40 items in this practice paper. Read each item carefully, then circle the letter with the correct answer. There is only one correct answer for each item.

For items 1 to 3, select the word that best completes the statement.

1 Tree is to trunk as flower is to …. …../1

 A seed

 B petal

 C stem

 D soil

2 Orange is to peel as egg is to …. …../1

 A shell

 B hen

 C yolk

 D juice

3 Perfume is to nose as music is to …. …../1

 A note

 B listen

 C tune

 D ear

Practice paper 2

In items 4 and 5, which word does not belong in the group?

4 A barley ...../1
   B hay
   C wheat
   D oats

5 A brush ...../1
   B sweep
   C scrub
   D comb

For items 6 and 7, select the most appropriate pair of words to complete each sentence.

6 There is no need to dress … for this occasion, casual … will do. ...../1
   A formally; clothes
   B formally; cloths
   C formerly; clothes
   D formerly; cloths

7 The shop … seem … with their job. ...../1
   A assistance; bored
   B assistance; board
   C assistants; bored
   D assistants; board

Practice paper 2

Each group below has words that are alike in some way. Use them to answer items 8 and 9.

8 | sorrow   grieve   mourn   anguish | ...../1

Which of the following is NOT like the words in the group above?

A   agony

B   lament

C   elation

D   despair

9 | frugal   economical   stingy   miserly | ...../1

Which of the following is NOT like the words in the group above?

A   thrifty

B   stingy

C   mean

D   generous

Read the passage below carefully, then use it to answer item 10 below.

> Audrey, Alex and Arthur love doing crossword puzzles. All the puzzles are the same level of difficulty. Audrey is the quickest. Alex does four every day. It takes Arthur two days to do the same number of crossword puzzles as Alex does in one day. Audrey does three more crossword puzzles per day than Alex.

10 If the above statements are true, this must mean that only one of the following statements can be true. Which one? Circle the statement you believe must be true.

A   Alex completes 12 crosswords in two days.

B   Arthur does nine crossword puzzles in three days.

C   Audrey does 14 crossword puzzles in two days.

D   Alex is the slowest at completing the crossword puzzles.

Practice paper 2

For items 11 to 13, circle the option that is an essential element of the word in bold.

11 train
A locomotive
B cargo
C ticket
D berth

...../1

12 pencil
A paper
B wood
C lead
D eraser

...../1

13 hospital
A doctor
B receptionist
C cafeteria
D patients

...../1

For items 14 and 15, select the word that comes next in the sequence.

14 flat, flatten; dear, endear; moist, moisten; pure, ...

A impure
B purification
C purify
D purifier

...../1

15 pack, package; press, pressure; grow, growth; declare, ...

A declaration
B declares
C declaring
D declared

...../1

Read the passages below carefully, then answer items 16 to 19.

Passage 1
The artificial environment that virtual reality creates makes it easy to get together and share experiences with strangers. You are also able to see, hear and feel details about places that you cannot get to visit otherwise. For example, through virtual reality you can stand on the peak of Mount Everest or ride the scariest rollercoaster at an amusement park.

Passage 2
How do people learn to function in the real world when they and the strangers they meet are pretending to be someone else? Virtual reality imitates the world but is not natural or real. While virtual reality makes it possible to have different experiences, people should limit their use of it and experience the real world with real people instead.

16 An appropriate title for Passage 1 is … ...../1

    A The disadvantages of virtual reality

    B The pros and cons of virtual reality

    C The concerns of virtual reality

    D The benefits of virtual reality

17 Which of the following phrases from Passage 2 supports the idea that virtual reality is an artificial environment? ...../1

    i. 'How do people learn to function in the real world when they and the strangers they meet are pretending to be someone else?'

    ii. 'Virtual reality imitates the real world but is not natural or real.'

    iii. '… virtual reality makes it possible to have different experiences …'

    iv. '… people should limit their use of it …'

        A i and ii

        B ii and iii

        C iii and iv

        D iv and i

18 Examples are used in Passage 1 to … ...../1

   A explain the weaknesses of virtual reality.

   B show the exciting things that people can experience through virtual reality.

   C prove that virtual reality is unnatural.

   D suggest that virtual reality is better than real world experiences.

19 Why does the writer ask the question at the beginning of Passage 2? ...../1

   A To confirm that strangers can share unusual experiences with each other

   B To promote the use of virtual reality to experience unfamiliar things

   C To disagree with the usefulness of virtual reality for people

   D To suggest that virtual reality can be dangerous and misleading

Read the passage below carefully, then use it to answer item 20.

> Zoe, Marcus, Anika, Tia and Chris take part in a sponsored silence to raise money for charity. They all begin at ten o'clock in the morning. Marcus speaks after 90 minutes. Zoe ends her silence at noon. Chris is silent for twice as long as Marcus. Tia starts speaking 15 minutes after Marcus. Anika is silent for less time than Zoe.

20 If the statements above are true, this must mean that only one of the following statements can be true. Which one? Circle the statement you believe must be true. ...../1

   A Zoe raises the most money for charity.

   B Zoe and Marcus speak at the same time.

   C Anika finds it the most difficult to remain silent.

   D Chris is silent for one hour longer than Zoe.

Practice paper 2

For item 21, select the number that completes the sequence.

21 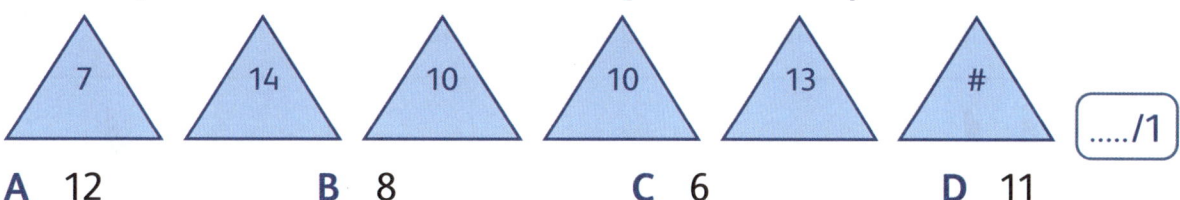   ...../1

A 12   B 8   C 6   D 11

Examine the pattern below. Use it to answer item 22.

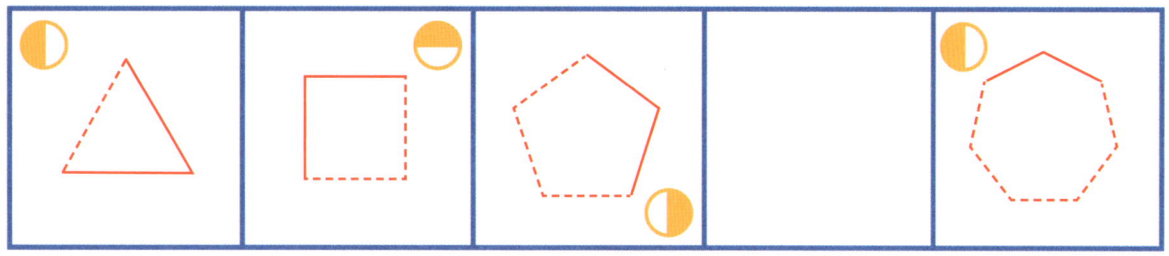

22 Circle the answer that completes the pattern.   ...../1

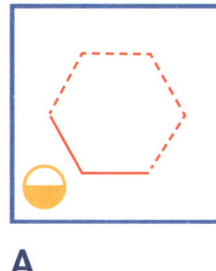 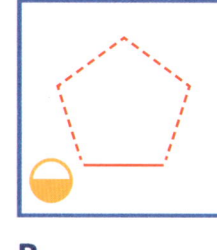 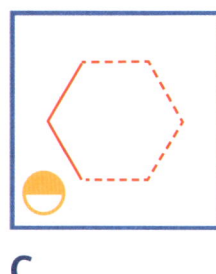 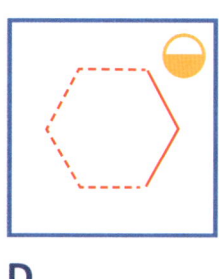

A   B   C   D

Look at the three groups labelled, D, E, F. Establish the relationship in group D. The same operation is used in group E and group F. Use the operation to find the missing number in group F in item 23.

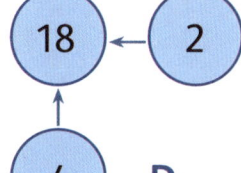 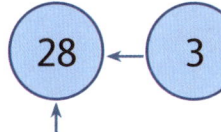 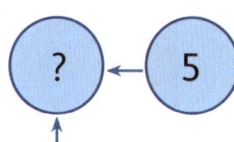

23 D (4 [18] 2)   ...../1
E (5 [28] 3)
F (7 [?] 5)

   A 54

   B 48

   C 56

   D 35

Practice paper 2

24 Gayle represented the following items from her classroom on a bar chart. Which bar chart best represents the information?

..../1

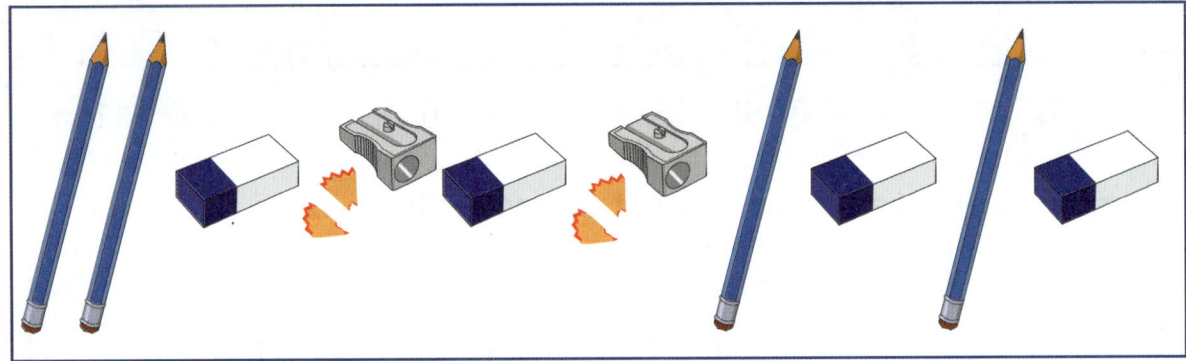

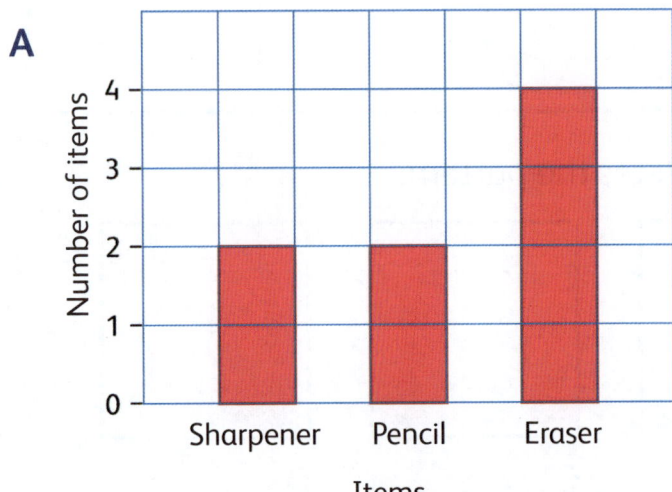

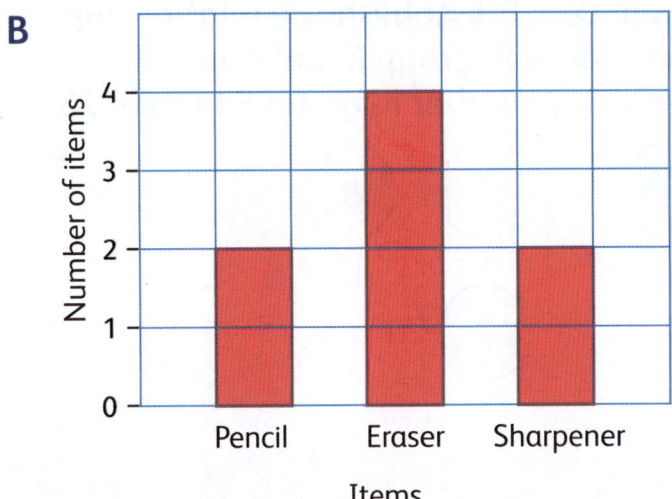

Practice paper 2

C
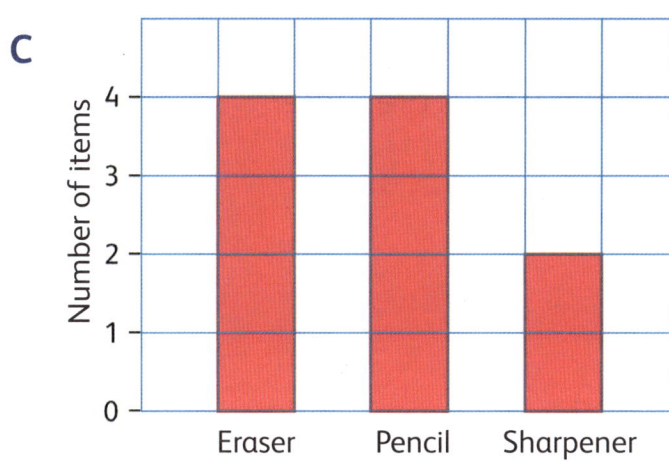

D
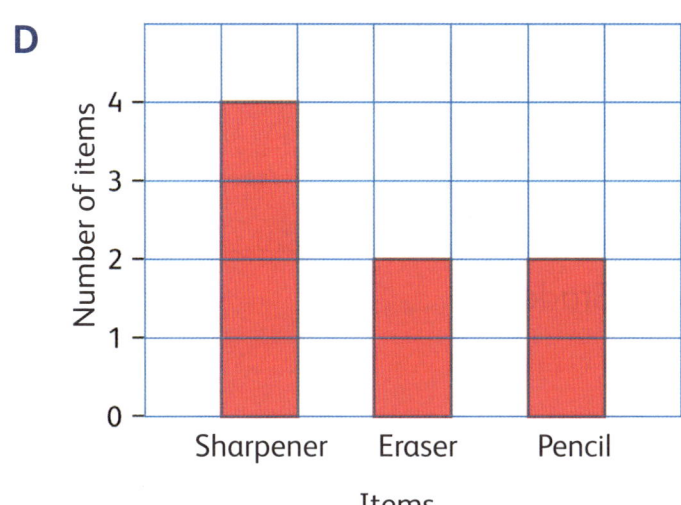

25 The rectangle below consists of 28 squares. If $\frac{1}{4}$ of the squares were shaded, how many squares would be shaded?   ..../1

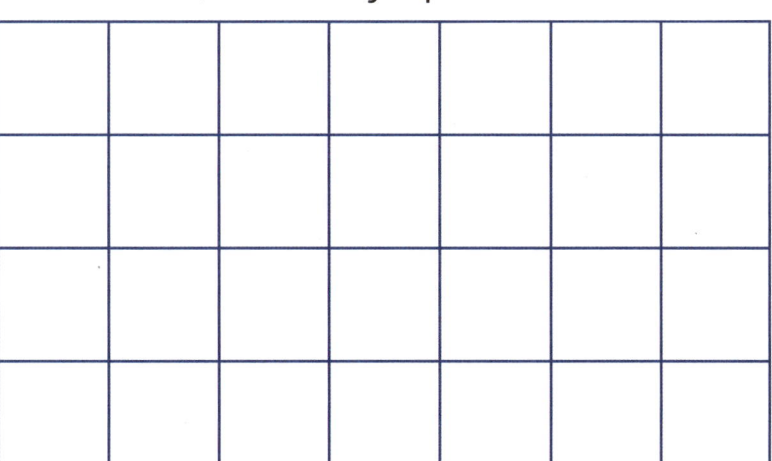

A 7

B 8

C 9

D 14

89

Practice paper 2

26 In a gymnastics club, there are 8 girls for every 3 boys. There are 55 children in the club. How many boys are there? ...../1

- A 15 boys
- B 11 boys
- C 20 boys
- D 24 boys

For items 27 to 30, use the table below, which gives details of the sports played by the learners in Grade 6.

	Play tennis	Do not play tennis
Play hockey	17	7
Do not play hockey	15	11

27 How many learners are there in Grade 6? ...../1

- A 48
- B 49
- C 50
- D 51

28 How many of the learners play tennis? ...../1

- A 32
- B 24
- C 18
- D 34

29 What percentage of the learners in Grade 6 do not play either tennis or hockey? ...../1

- A 11%
- B 22%
- C 44%
- D 26%

30 How many more learners play tennis than play hockey?

A 5

B 6

C 7

D 8

31 Three number cards are shown below. The cards can be placed together to make three-digit numbers, for example, 497.

4 7 9 → 4 9 7

How many different three-digit odd numbers, including 497, can be made using these cards?

A 3

B 4

C 5

D 6

32 The bar chart shows the heights of young plants.

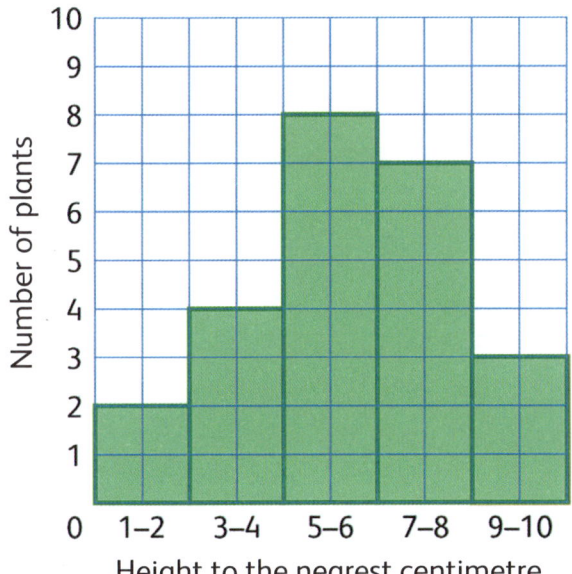

Height to the nearest centimetre

Which statement must be true?

A One plant is 1 cm tall.

B Three plants are at least 10 cm tall.

C One-sixth of the plants are either 3 or 4 cm tall.

D There are 20 plants in the study.

Practice paper 2

33 In seven years' time, Sandy will be three times as old as she was a year ago. How old is Sandy now?   ...../1

   A 4

   B 5

   C 6

   D 7

34 A farmer has 24 sheep and 16 cows that he needs to move in a trailer.   ...../1

   The trailer can carry up to 7 sheep or up to 3 cows.

   The sheep and cows cannot be mixed when being moved.

   How many journeys does the trailer need to take to move all the sheep and cows?

   A 10

   B 12

   C 17

   D 20

35 What fraction, in its lowest terms, of the regular octagon has been coloured?   ...../1

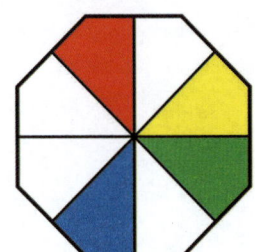

   A $\frac{4}{8}$

   B $\frac{4}{9}$

   C $\frac{1}{2}$

   D $\frac{1}{3}$

92

36 The pictogram below shows the number of boys and girls in Grade 6.

Boys	OOOOOOOO
Girls	OOOOOOOOOOOO

One symbol O represents two learners.

What is the ratio of the number of boys to girls in Grade 6, written in its simplest form?

A 4:6

B 2:3

C 1:2

D 8:12

37 A magazine has 60 pages and 18 of the pages are printed in colour. What percentage of the pages is printed in colour?

A 20%

B 30%

C 18%

D 36%

38 The learners in a class were asked to choose a favourite 'supper' from the lunch shop menu.

	Fish	Chicken	Burger
Boys	4	4	5
Girls	5	?	6

If there are six more girls in the class than there are boys, how many girls chose chicken?

A 5

B 6

C 7

D 8

Practice paper 2

39 The grid contains the numbers 1 to 9. ...../1

The row and column totals are printed in white on blue.
What number goes in the shaded box?

A 6

B 7

C 8

D 9

40 The first three patterns in a sequence are shown below. ...../1

pattern 1   pattern 2   pattern 3

How many small triangles will there be in pattern 6?

A 24

B 28

C 32

D 36

Record your score ...../40

Practice paper 3

General instructions

There are 40 items in this practice paper. Read each item carefully, then circle the letter with the correct answer. There is only one correct answer for each item.

For items 1 to 3, select the word that best completes the statement.

1 Fall is to descend as scale is to …. ...../1
   A measure
   B fish
   C grade
   D climb

2 Brave is to courageous as cowardly is to …. ...../1
   A fearful
   B timid
   C week
   D mild

3 Five is to pentagon as seven is to …. ...../1
   A hexagon
   B polygon
   C septagon
   D heptagon

Practice paper 3

In items 4 and 5, which word does not belong in the group?

4 A explore ...../1

   B discover

   C explain

   D seek

5 A raise ...../1

   B lift

   C elevate

   D pull

For items 6 and 7, select the most appropriate pair of words to complete each sentence.

6 The gardener fell into a … in the backyard and was not discovered until … when the family returned home. ...../1

   A whole; later

   B hole; later

   C hole; latter

   D whole; latter

7 The driver … that area just before … struck the tree and it fell across the road. ...../1

   A past; lightening

   B passed; lightening

   C passed; lightning

   D past; lightning

Each group below has words that are alike in some way. Use them to answer items 8 and 9.

8 think   consider   muse   ponder   ...../1

Which of the following is NOT like the words in the group above?

A contemplate

B ignore

C mull

D reflect

9 capable   accomplished   qualified   skilled   ...../1

Which of the following is NOT like the words in the group above?

A novice

B adept

C mastered

D competent

Read the passage below carefully, then use it to answer item 10 below.

Ali, Ryan and Tom all enjoy different sports. Tom prefers most team games. Ryan likes individual sports. Ali only plays football and rugby. The boys have activities on a Tuesday.

10 If the above statements are true, this must mean that only one of the following statements can be true. Which one? Circle the statement you believe must be true.

A Tom and Ali enjoy playing rugby.

B Tom loves playing football.

C Ryan plays badminton on a Tuesday.

D Both Tom and Ali enjoy team sports.

Practice paper 3

For items 11 to 13, circle the option that is an essential element of the word in bold.

11 aeroplane   A   wing   ...../1

B   window

C   headphones

D   food tray

12 building   A   walls   ...../1

B   stairs

C   doors

D   deck

13 shirt   A   buttons   ...../1

B   fabric

C   pattern

D   pocket

For items 14 and 15, select the word that comes next in the sequence.

14 abundant, sparse; admit, repudiate; blame, praise; descend, .../1

A   decline

B   shield

C   oust

D   ascend

15 read, readable; obey, obedient; enjoy, .../1

A   rejoice

B   enjoys

C   enjoyable

D   enjoyed

98

Practice paper 3

Read the passage below carefully, then answer items 16 to 19.

Hope is the thing with feathers

By Emily Dickinson

Hope is the thing with feathers
That perches in the soul,
And sings the tune without the words,
And never stops at all,

And sweetest in the gale is heard;
And sore must be the storm
That could abash* the little bird
That kept so many warm.

I've heard it in the chillest land,
And on the strangest sea;
Yet, never, in extremity,
It asked a crumb of me.

* abash – deflate, humiliate

16 What is the figure of speech in the first line of the poem? ...../1

    A simile

    B metaphor

    C personification

    D alliteration

17 What picture comes to mind after reading the first stanza of the poem? ...../1

    A 'A bird on the branch of a tree'

    B 'A ghostly person sitting on a chair'

    C 'A musician playing a musical instrument'

    D 'Someone that cannot stop moving'

18 In the poem, 'And sore must be the storm / That could abash the little bird' means … …/1

    A   that hope is always present when people face challenges.

    B   the challenges of life that could cause a person to give up.

    C   that hope only lasts for a short time when there are challenges.

    D   the challenges of life always defeat the hope that people have.

19 Which of the following lines shows that hope stays alive even in unexpected circumstances? …/1

    A   'That perches in the soul'

    B   'That kept so many warm'

    C   'I've heard it in the chillest land'

    D   'Yet, never, in extremity'

Read the passage below carefully, then use it to answer item 20.

> Helena, Eve, Marcus and Rohan complete a survey about how they get to school. Eve and Rohan both catch the number 10 bus. Marcus usually walks to school but gets a lift if it is raining. Helena gets a lift every day because her father works near the school. Marcus and Rohan live in the same street. Rohan lives nearer the school than Helena.

20 If the statements above are true, this must mean that only one of the following statements can be true. Which one? Circle the statement you believe must be true. …/1

    A   Helena lives further from the school than Eve.

    B   Nobody in Rohan's family drives a car.

    C   If it is sunny, Marcus walks to school.

    D   Helena lives too far from the school to walk.

Practice paper 3

For item 21, select the number that completes the sequence.

21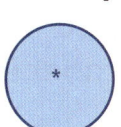

..../1

A 121
B 8
C 96
D 100

Examine the pattern below. Use it to answer item 22.

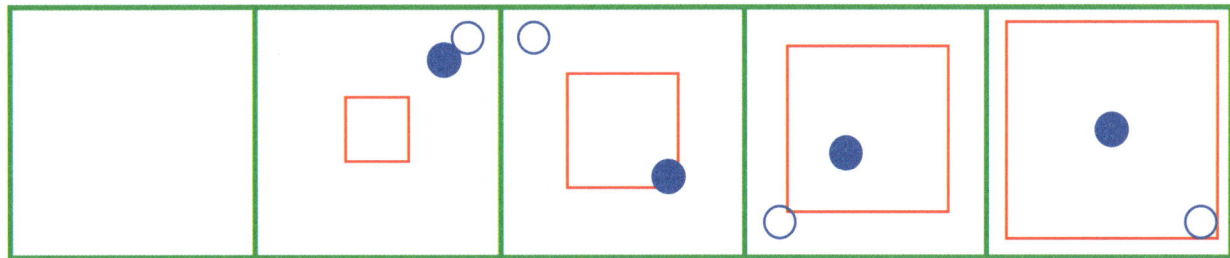

22 Circle the answer that completes the sequence.

..../1

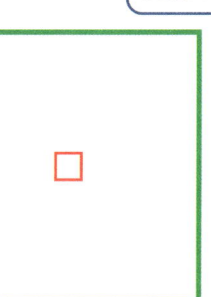 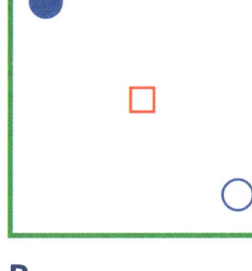 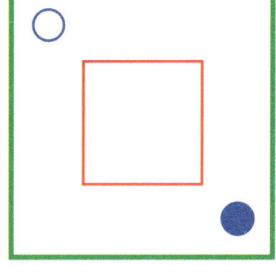

A   B   C   D

Practice paper 3

Look at the three groups labelled, J, K, L. Establish the relationship in group J. The same operation is used in group K and group L. Use the operation to find the missing number in group L in item 23.

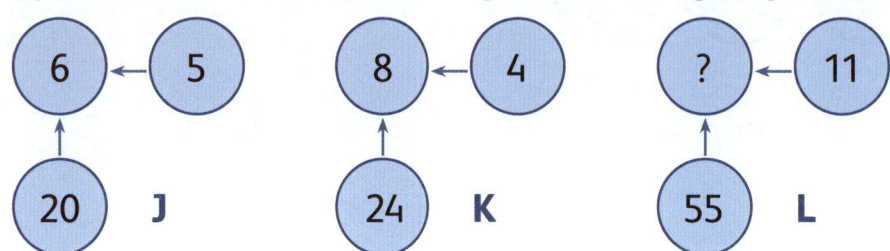

23 J (20 [6] 5)
K (24 [8] 4)
L (55 [?] 11)

..../1

A 65

B 7

C 10

D 66

24 Which bar chart best represents the information below?

..../1

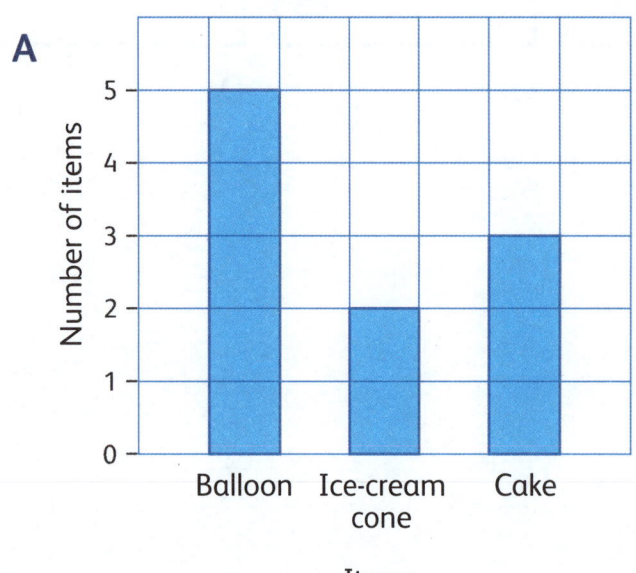

Practice paper 3

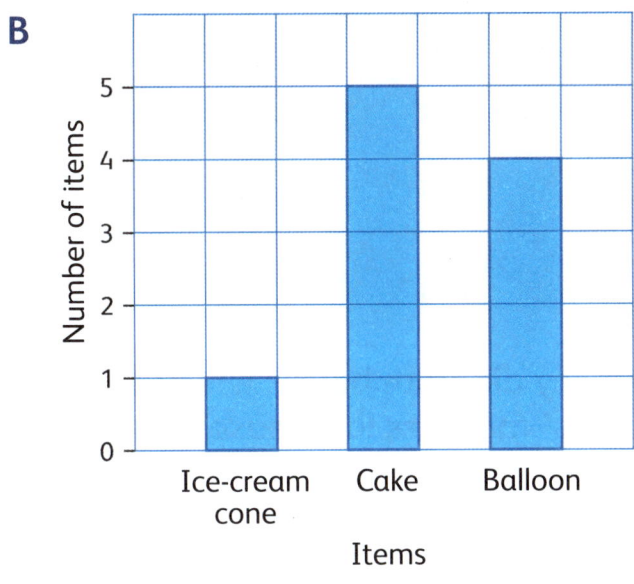

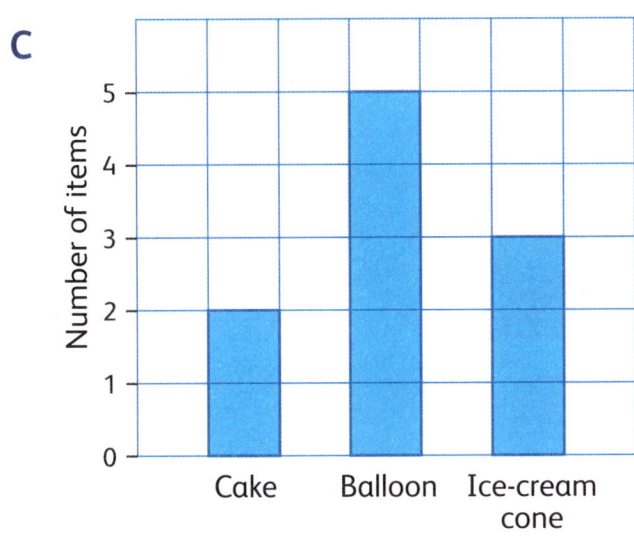

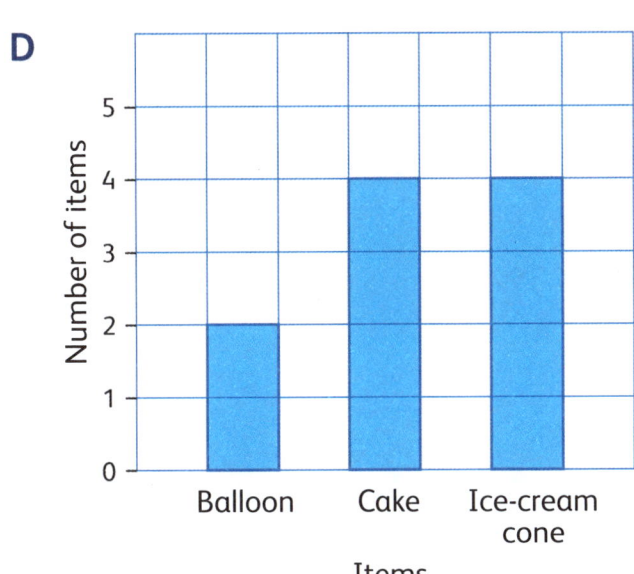

103

Practice paper 3

25 Ajani is reading a book. He has read 135 pages, which is $\frac{3}{8}$ of the book. How many pages does the book have altogether?

- A 450 pages
- B 360 pages
- C 320 pages
- D 400 pages

For items 26 and 27, use the frequency diagram below, which shows the number of goals scored in Terriers' matches last season.

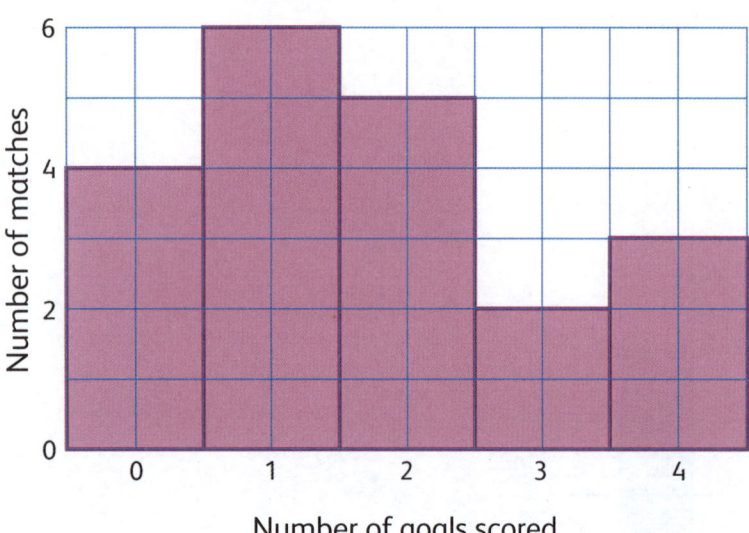

Number of goals scored

26 How many matches did the Terriers play last season?

- A 20
- B 4
- C 10
- D 16

27 How many goals were scored last season?

- A 38
- B 34
- C 20
- D 36

28 Which number is closest to 5? ...../1

   A 4.9

   B 5.05

   C 4.96

   D 5.1

29 In which number below does the 7 have the greatest value? ...../1

   A 7.98

   B 7 653

   C 96,735

   D 0.078

30 Robert has 80 identical bricks with a total mass of 4 kg. What is the mass of one brick? ...../1

   A 20 g

   B 50 g

   C 200 g

   D 500 g

31 The 16 learners in a class recorded the numbers of brothers and sisters they have. ...../1

Number of brothers and sisters	Number of learners
0	3
1	5
2	6
3	2

The teacher invites all 16 learners and all their brothers and sisters to a party. How many children does the teacher invite to the party?

   A 22

   B 42

   C 48

   D 39

Practice paper 3

32 When the spinner is spun, which one of the following statements is true?

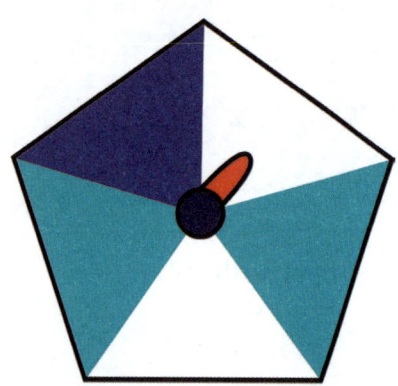

- **A** The spinner is most likely to land on white.
- **B** The spinner has a more than even chance of landing on light blue.
- **C** The spinner is as likely to land on white as to land on light blue.
- **D** The spinner is least likely to land on light blue.

33 What is the area of the shape?

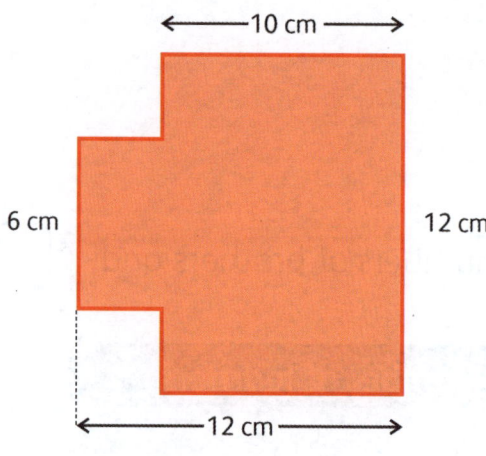

Not to scale

- **A** 124 cm²
- **B** 132 cm²
- **C** 138 cm²
- **D** 140 cm²

34 A piece of wire is bent to form a regular hexagon with sides of length 8 cm.

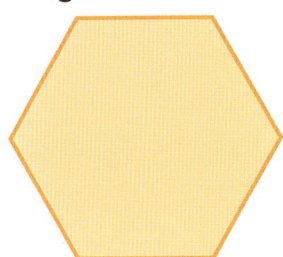

The wire is straightened out and then bent again to form a square. What is the length of a side of the square?

A 8 cm

B 10 cm

C 12 cm

D 14 cm

35 The diagram shows part of a jumbled multiplication square.

×	7	5	8	6
9	63	45	72	54
3	21	15		18
8		15	64	48
3	28	20	32	24

Which two numbers are missing?

A 24, 63

B 56, 24

C 63, 32

D 56, 32

Practice paper 3

36 Rachael multiplied her favourite number by 5, then subtracted 5 and finally multiplied by 3.

The result was 60.

What is Rachael's favourite number?

    A 3

    B 4

    C 5

    D 6

37 In a group of 60 children, 24 are boys. What percentage of the group are girls?

    A 32%

    B 36%

    C 60%

    D 72%

38 At Grange School, 123 children walk to school, 39 are taken by car and 18 are taken in a minibus.

How many children are at Grange School?

    A 175

    B 180

    C 185

    D 190

39 It is known that 18.5 × 3.8 = 70.3

Using this fact, what is the value of 140.6 ÷ 18.5?

    A 1.9

    B 7.4

    C 3.8

    D 7.6

40 On the grid below, three of the corners of a square are marked with crosses.

..../1

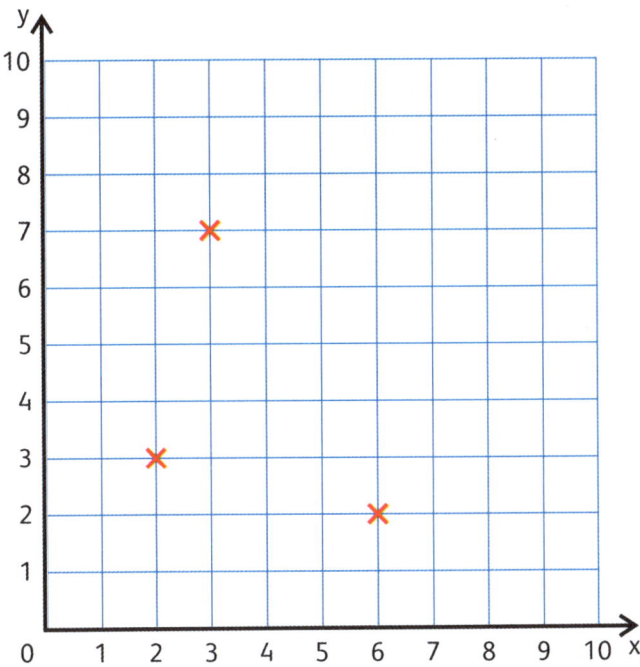

What are the coordinates of the fourth corner of the square?

A (6, 7)

B (7, 6)

C (8, 8)

D (7, 7)

Record your score ....../40

Practice paper 4

General instructions

There are 40 items in this practice paper. Read each item carefully, then circle the letter with the correct answer. There is only one correct answer for each item.

For items 1 to 3, select the word that best completes the statement.

1 Team is to group as teem is to …. ...../1

    A swarm

    B term

    C sport

    D pair

2 Wing is to fly as tail is to …. ...../1

    A feather

    B scale

    C balance

    D fur

3 However is to but as also is to …. ...../1

    A moreover

    B meanwhile

    C consequently

    D although

Practice paper 4

In items 4 and 5, which word does not belong in the group?

4 A aid
    B help
    C bandage
    D support

5 A fume
    B smoulder
    C scorch
    D seethe

For items 6 and 7, select the most appropriate pair of words to complete each sentence.

6 The president said a policy change is … and he expects some people to … the party.

    A imminent; desert
    B imminent; dessert
    C eminent; desert
    D eminent; dessert

7 These are very … conditions, and we will need to … with caution.

    A constricting; proceed
    B constricting; precede
    C constructing; proceed
    D constructing; precede

Practice paper 4

Each group below has words that are alike in some way.
Use them to answer items 8 and 9.

8   cost   fee   rate   charge   ....../1

Which of the following is NOT like the words in the group above?

A profit

B price

C expense

D tariff

9   photograph   image   likeness   picture   ....../1

Which of the following is NOT like the words in the group above?

A portrait

B snapshot

C print

D camera

Read the passage below carefully, then use it to answer item 10 below.

> Mammals are one of six main groups of animals. Mammals are warm blooded. Polar bears are large white Arctic bears. Bears are mammals with warm, hairy coats. Most mammals have hair on their bodies. Mammals live everywhere. Camels live in hot areas. Bats can live in caves and fly in the air.

10 If the above statements are true, this must mean that only one of the following statements can be true. Circle the statement you believe must be true.   ....../1

A Bats are in the bird group.

B Mammals all have hairy coats.

C Polar bears are mammals.

D All mammals are bears.

For items 11 to 13, circle the option that is an essential element of the word in bold.

11 calendar
- A months
- B birthdays
- C pictures
- D holidays

..../1

12 portrait
- A easel
- B paint
- C canvas
- D palette

..../1

13 exercise
- A gym
- B instructor
- C equipment
- D movement

..../1

For items 14 and 15, select the word that comes next in the sequence.

14 youth, youthful; amuse, amusing; play, ...
- A played
- B playful
- C plays
- D played

..../1

15 incredible, amazing; terrible, dreadful; weep, cry; ruin, ...
- A raze
- B erect
- C receive
- D evade

..../1

Practice paper 4

Read the advertisement below, then answer items 16 to 19.

JAMUSEMENT WORLD

Love the thrill of a rollercoaster ride?

Want a summer to remember without the extra cost of a plane ticket to Florida?

10% off with student ID

Jamaica's only world-class amusement park has something for the entire family.

From teacups for the toddlers to rollercoaster acrobatics for the adrenaline addicts!

Great summer memories are just a ticket away.

Visit our website at www.jamusementworld.com or call 876-555-1234

---

16 The question 'Love the thrill of a rollercoaster ride?' is used to …. ..../1

    A appeal to people who like to visit amusement parks

    B show that rollercoaster rides are entertaining

    C remind people who love rollercoasters of the dangers

    D convince visitors to the park that rollercoasters are safe

17 When do you think the amusement park is open? ...../1

　　A　on weekends

　　B　school holidays

　　C　all year round

　　D　summer time

18 Which line in the advertisement has the same purpose as the line '… without the extra cost of a plane ticket to Florida?' ...../1

　　A　'Want a summer to remember?'

　　B　'10% off with student ID'

　　C　'Jamaica's only world class amusement park …'

　　D　'… summer memories are just a ticket away'

19 'teacups for the toddlers' and 'acrobatics for the adrenaline addicts' are examples of … ...../1

　　A　simile

　　B　metaphor

　　C　personification

　　D　alliteration

Read the passage below carefully, then use it to answer item 20.

> Michael, Ross and Lucy all have pets. Michael and Lucy both have a dog. Lucy and Ross both have a cat. Michael and Ross have a guinea pig. Ross has a goldfish.

20 If the above statements are true, this must mean that only one of the following statements is true. Which one? Circle the statement you believe must be true. ...../1

　　A　Ross is afraid of dogs.

　　B　Ross has three pets.

　　C　Lucy has a pet guinea pig.

　　D　Michael does not like goldfish.

Practice paper 4

For item 21, select the number that completes the sequence.

21 | 7 | 8 | 11 | 16 | 15 | 32 | # |

....../1

A 21

B 19

C 36

D 30

Examine the pattern below. Use it to answer item 22.

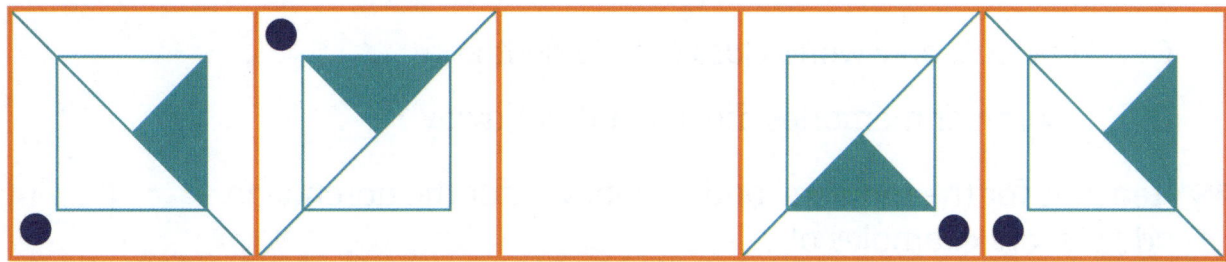

22 Circle the answer that completes the pattern.

....../1

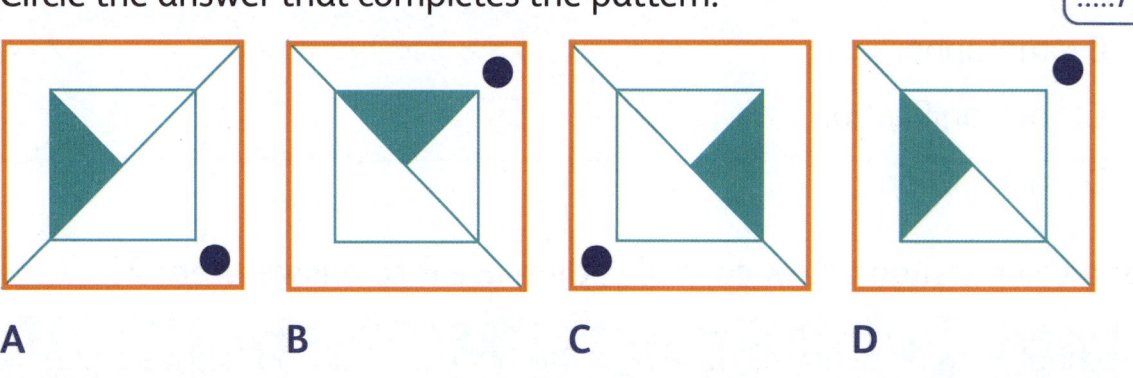

A   B   C   D

Look at the three groups labelled, O, P, Q. Establish the relationship in group O. The same operation is used in group P and group Q. Use the operation to find the missing number in group Q in item 23.

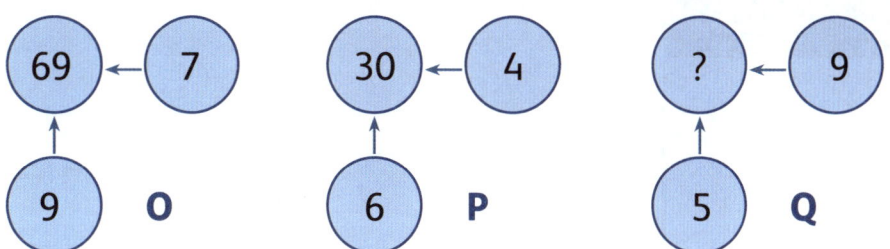

23 O (9 [69] 7)
P (6 [30] 4)
Q (5 [?] 9)

A 54

B 51

C 20

D 10

…../1

24 Use the clue to find the correct number.

This number is eight times the product of six and two.

A 112

B 108

C 96

D 88

…../1

25 There are between 80 and 90 biscuits in a biscuit tin. Tommy eats exactly $\frac{1}{4}$ of the biscuits and Billy eats exactly $\frac{1}{7}$ of them. How many biscuits were in the tin to start with?

A 81

B 84

C 85

D 87

…../1

Practice paper 4

26 Which multiplication in this multiplication square is incorrect? ..../1

×	7	5	8	3
4	28	20	32	12
9	63	45	72	27
6	42	30	46	18
12	84	60	96	36

A 8 × 6

B 7 × 12

C 8 × 9

D 5 × 12

27 Which number between 100 and 130 is a multiple of both 8 and 7? ..../1

A 126

B 128

C 112

D 102

28 Ted thinks of a number. He divides it by 6 and then subtracts 4. The result is 3. What was Ted's original number? ..../1

A 16

B 24

C 36

D 42

118

29 What number should go in the box?

14 + 14 + 14 + 14 + 14 + 14 = ☐ × 12

A 14

B 84

C 12

D 16

30 A local pet shop sells tropical fish. A group of learners counted the fish and plotted a bar chart to show the results.

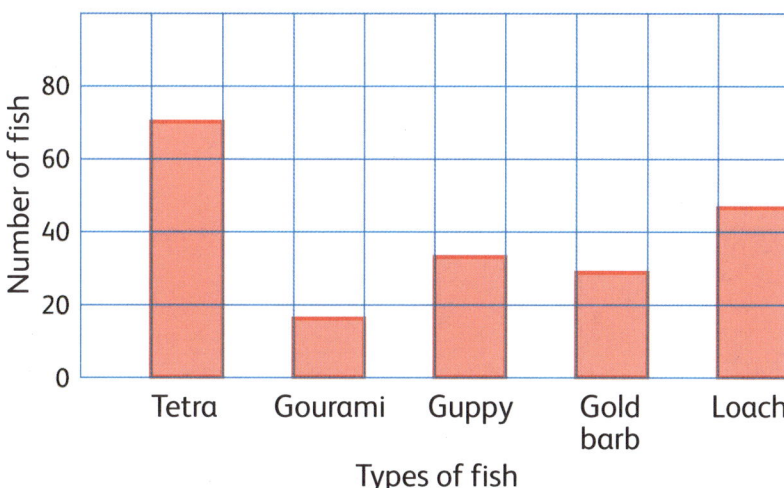

How many more tetras are there than gold barbs?

A 40

B 35

C 30

D 25

31 What shape do these clues describe?

I have two pairs of parallel sides.

My opposite sides are equal in length.

I do not have any right angles.

A a square

B a rectangle

C a trapezium

D a parallelogram

Practice paper 4

Items 32 to 35 are concerned with Zara's counters, shown below.

32 What fraction of Zara's counters are dark blue? ...../1

A $\frac{1}{2}$

B $\frac{1}{3}$

C $\frac{3}{8}$

D $\frac{2}{3}$

33 What is the ratio of light blue : white counters? ...../1

A 1 : 2

B 4 : 3

C 2 : 1

D 3 : 1

34 Zara puts the counters in her pocket and then picks one counter at random. What is the probability that she will not pick a light blue counter? ...../1

A $\frac{1}{2}$

B $\frac{2}{5}$

C $\frac{4}{9}$

D $\frac{5}{9}$

35 Zara puts back the counter she picked from her pocket. She loses one white counter and cannot find it. She picks one of the remaining counters from her pocket at random. What is the probability that the counter picked is dark blue? ...../1

A $\frac{1}{4}$

B $\frac{3}{8}$

C $\frac{3}{4}$

D $\frac{5}{8}$

36 Use these clues to work out Brianne's favourite number. ..../1

It is between 50 and 90.

It is a multiple of 8.

It is also a multiple of 6.

   A 56

   B 64

   C 72

   D 80

37 Sam thought of a number, multiplied it by 4 and then subtracted 5. ..../1
The result was 23. What number did Sam think of?

   A 7

   B 8

   C $6\frac{1}{2}$

   D $7\frac{1}{2}$

38 How many letters in the word MATHS have only one line ..../1
of symmetry?

MATHS

   A 1

   B 2

   C 3

   D 4

Practice paper 4

39 The diagram below shows the results when the learners in a school were asked if they owned a bicycle.

Own a bicycle	47	37
Do not own a bicycle	23	28
	Boys	Girls

How many more learners own a bicycle than do not own a bicycle?

A 43

B 13

C 33

D 24

..../1

40 The pictogram below shows the number of pets seen by a vet during one week.

One symbol represents two pets.

How many more dogs than cats did he see?

A 3

B 5

C 6

D 7

..../1

Record your score ....../40

Exam tips and guidelines

Here are some tips and guidelines in case you feel anxious and overwhelmed as you get closer to the day of your exam.

In the months leading up to your exam:
- Build your critical thinking skills in all subject areas. What you learn in the other subjects will help you to understand the test items on the Ability Test paper. You will also be able to link ideas and use logical reasoning to find the correct answers.
- Ask your teacher to go over the steps for the item styles that you don't quite understand. You can also read through the steps in this volume and complete the worksheets.
- Pace yourself. Understand one item style before you move on to the next.
- Attempt the first practice paper, when you feel confident.
- Look at the items that you did not score a mark for, then review the notes and steps for those item styles. Attempt to answer the same items a second time. If you still are not able to find the correct answer, ask your teacher for help.

One week before the exam:
- Revise the item styles and work through the practice papers in both Volume 1 and Volume 2.
- Explain to a classmate who does not understand an item style.
- Practise!

The day before the exam:
- Make sure you are well rested. Try to relax the afternoon before your exam and get a good night's sleep.
- Be around people who have a positive attitude.
- Prepare your exam kit with pencils, pens, erasers and whatever else you are allowed to take with you to the exam.
- Do not try any new foods.

Exam tips and guidelines

The day of the exam:
- Eat your usual breakfast.
- Make sure you have your exam kit.
- Get to the exam location early so that you are relaxed and comfortable.
- Do your best!

Feeling anxious and overwhelmed before an exam is perfectly normal. Take a deep breath and remember that you have been preparing for it for months, so just do your best.